PRACTICAL
BIRDING

Peter Ryan

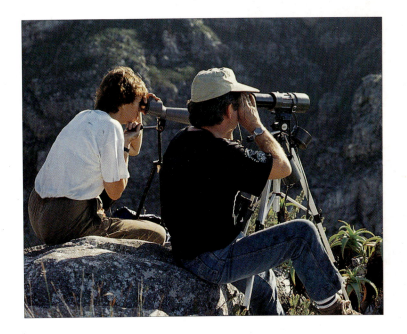

Acknowledgements

This book is the synthesis of many years' birding. I'm grateful to all my friends and colleagues who helped me develop as a birder. Phil Hockey, Ian Sinclair, John Graham, Callan Cohen, Claire Spottiswoode and Trevor Hardaker provided useful comments on the text. My thanks also go to Pippa Parker and the Struik team for carrying this project to fruition.

Struik Publishers
(A division of The New Holland Publishing
   Group (South Africa) (Pty) Ltd)
Cornelis Struik House
80 McKenzie Street
Cape Town 8001
South Africa
www.struik.co.za

First published in 2001

10 9 8 7 6 5 4 3 2 1

Copyright in text © Peter Ryan 2001
Copyright in photographs © individual
   photographers as credited below, 2001
Copyright in illustrations © Struik Publishers
   and Peter Ryan 2001
Copyright in maps © Struik Publishers 2001
Copyright in published edition © Struik
   Publishers 2001

Publishing manager: Pippa Parker
Managing editor: Helen de Villiers
Editor: Jeanne Hromnik
Designer: Dominic Robson
Cover designer: Robin Cox
Illustrator: Ian Lusted

Reproduction by Hirt & Carter (Pty) Ltd,
   Cape Town
Printed and bound by Trident Press (Pty) Ltd

All rights reserved. No part of this publication may be reproduced, stored in a retrieval system, or transmitted, in any form or by any means, electronic, mechanical, photocopying, recording or otherwise, without the written permission of the copyright owner(s).

ISBN 1 86872 608 8

Photograhic credits
Photographs are labelled by page number from top to bottom and from left to right.
Photo Access = PA, SIL = Struik Image Library, ABPL = Anthony Bannister Photo Library

Front Cover: Top left, A Froneman; right, S Adey/SIL; bottom, A Bannister/ABPL; backround image, A Bannister/ABPL
Back cover: Top, R du Toit; bottom, J Haigh/SIL

S Adey/SIL: 79; Gallo/W Tarboton: 6; Gallo/A Bannister: 62; T Camacho: 33a, 56a, 69c, 85b;
T Camacho/SIL: 33, 92; P Chadwick: 29a, 36, 52b, 56b; R de la Harpe/DD Photography: 37, 50, 59c;
NJ Dennis: 21d, 29b, 31, 49b, 53, 55, 57a, 58, 68a; NJ Dennis/SIL: 38a; R du Toit: 3a, 21b, 59a, 70;
A Froneman: 21a, 21c, 21f, 22a, 22b, 24a, 49a, 52a, 59b, 60b, 68b, 69b;
Gallo/NJ Dennis: 45; Gallo/W Tarboton: 57b; J Haigh/SIL: 9, 14, 28, 38b, 75, 76, 86;
R Meyer: 44, 48, 80, 87; PA/JJ Brooks: 25a, 60a; PA/T Carew: 69a; PA/J Cummins: 78;
PA/R Gush: 51a; PA/HPH Photography: 4, 16, 24b; PA/P Steyn: title page; PA/A Wilson: 25b;
PA/B&L Worsley: 5b, 85a; C Paterson-Jones: 21e, 24d, 51b, 54; D Richards: 73;
P Ryan: 5a, 23a, 23b, 23c, 40, 42, 43, 61, 64, 67, 71, 72; C Spottiswoode: 13; L Stanton: 89;
P Steyn: 63, 81; Swarovski Optik: 3b, 10, 12a,b & c, 74; W Tarboton: 24c, 46a, 82, 83

CONTENTS

1. Why watch birds? **4**

2. Basic equipment **9**

3. Getting to know birds **16**

4. Field skills **31**

5. Where to bird **43**

6. Birding socially **62**

7. Advanced birding **67**

8. Making a contribution to ornithology **81**

Addresses and other useful information **90**

New classification of birds **94**

Index **96**

WHY WATCH BIRDS?

People start watching birds for different reasons: they may see a spectacular bird, they may be press-ganged into it by friends or relatives, or they may simply run out of big and hairy mammals to 'tick off' in game reserves. Whatever the reason, once you start, you tend to become a dedicated birder because of the enjoyment you derive from this hobby.

Birds, like humans, mostly use visual cues to communicate. They are, thus, much more rewarding to observe than mammals, many of which communicate largely through their sense of smell. Ultimately, it is our ability to relate to birds that makes them so fascinating to observe; one has only to witness the universal appeal of penguins.

Birdwatching is a relatively new pursuit. Early naturalists learned just about everything they knew about birds from dead specimens. Indeed, many of the famous explorer-naturalists hardly ever observed the birds they described, relying, instead, on 'native' shooters to collect specimens. Birding as a hobby (and indeed modern ornithology) became possible only with the development of effective optical aids in the first half of the twentieth century. The other significant development that promoted birdwatching was the publication in the 1930s of the first field guides.

Since then, birding has grown out of all proportion. It is no longer the preserve of elderly eccentrics; there are now millions of people who watch birds around the world. It is even considered a trendy pastime in some circles, and attracts a large following of obsessive characters who literally live to see new birds. But don't be put off by the condescending attitudes and jargon of many 'experienced' birders. Birdwatching can be enjoyed at many levels, and doesn't require great sacrifice.

Wandering Albatross

There could hardly be a better place than southern Africa to nurture an interest in birds. Many southern African birds such as storks, hornbills, rollers and turacos (loeries) are large and colourful, making their identification easy. At the same time there are several tricky groups of birds such as larks, cisticolas and pipits that offer a challenge to more advanced birders.

Although it makes up only a fraction of the world's land area, southern Africa supports more than 950 bird species – some 10 per cent of the world's birds. Africa as a whole supports almost a quarter of all the bird species in the world. This diversity can be daunting when you first start out, but the rewards are great for those who persevere.

Perhaps the most important part of becoming a birder is that you become much more aware of the environment in which you live. Birds are good indicators of the state of the natural world, and most birdwatchers make excellent, environmentally aware citizens.

Birding ethics

A birder's primary concern is the bird's welfare, which supersedes every desire to see a particular species. Birds must not be chased or repeatedly flushed. Tape recordings of birdsong are to be used sparingly. Rare birds and birds that are breeding are to be treated with extra care. This applies especially to photographers, who often try to approach birds more closely than birders. It is of supreme importance that the bird's habitat is not damaged. Permission should be obtained when birding on private land.

White-starred Robin

WHY WATCH BIRDS?

BIRDING JARGON

As you read through this book, you will encounter some terms peculiar to birds and birding. Much of this birding jargon derives from the frenetic UK birding scene, immortalized by Bill Oddie in his *Little Black Bird Book* (Methuen, 1980), which should be required reading for anyone who wants to take up birding.

The following glossary defines some frequently used birding terms. It will give you an idea (fair warning?) of the road ahead.

alien (n) an exotic species, introduced by humans.
armchair tick (n) a new bird added to your life list on the basis of past sightings when subspecies are raised to species level by 'splitting'. There's no specific term for the more painful 'loss' of a species through 'lumping'. (*See* 'lump' and 'split'.)
atlas (v) to make species lists for specific areas and times for a bird atlas: 'I'm going atlasing this weekend.'
bins (n) binoculars. Also known as 'noccies' by the less than macho birder.
birder (n) a birdwatcher, more committed to the pursuit than the stereotyped little old ladies and retired military gentlemen that formed the popular image of a birdwatcher. (*See* 'dude'.)
bogey bird (n) a species (often fairly common) that eludes you despite considerable effort on your part.
budgie (n) a derogatory term for any parrot species; sometimes also used for any small bird.
clean up (v) to see all the birds available in an area (as identified by your 'hit list').
CMF (n) a truly spectacular bird; acronym for cosmic mind f@!*er. Many birders resort to foul language when attempting to describe their out-of-the-ordinary birding experiences.
cosmic (adj) a slightly less spectacular bird than a CMF.
dip (v) to miss out on a bird (a painful business!); a 'dipper' is one who dips out (also one of a group of birds that are famous for feeding underwater in streams and rivers).
dross (n) same as 'junk birds'.
dude (n) derogatory term for casual birdwatchers who are not prepared to risk death or make a 2:00 a.m. start for a chance at a 'lifer' or two.
duff gen (n) bad information. Can refer either to misidentified birds (especially rare species) or poor directions to a particular bird/site.
endemic (n) restricted-range species. Strictly speaking, the range should be defined (e.g. Namib endemic for species found only in the Namib Desert), but often used loosely at country or regional level. Within southern Africa an endemic is taken to mean any species restricted to the region.
fall (n) the arrival of a large number of 'migrants', which can often include some good 'vagrants'.

Rufous-eared Warbler: South African endemic

flush (v) to cause a bird to take flight (e.g. to see its wing pattern or merely to see it if it is hiding in dense vegetation).

flog (v) to bird an area intensively; often used when attempting to flush rails and other reluctant species from wetlands and marshes. Also termed 'thrashing' or 'burning up' an area.

grapevine (n) the informal network that alerts 'twitchers' that a rare bird is around.

grip (v) to see a bird, generally a rare or sought-after species. In competitive circles, you can 'grip off' your mates by seeing such a bird.

hard core (adj) going to great lengths, and considerable personal discomfort, to see a bird (e.g. driving non-stop for a day-and-a-half to lie motionless for hours in a mosquito-infested ditch to glimpse a rare reed warbler that looks just like every other reed warbler).

have (v) to see a bird, as in 'I've just had a Red-tailed Tropicbird'.

hit list (n) a list of wanted species for a given area/trip. (*See* 'wants'.)

irruption (n) an influx of a species outside its usual range. Some species are more prone to irrupt than are others.

junk bird (n) a common species. Can also be used to put down someone else's good sighting: 'Oh, that's a junk bird.' (But you are permitted to say this *only* if you have seen it at least once!)

LBJ (n) acronym of Little Brown Job; a 'dude' term for any small, drab bird.

lifer (n) a new bird, not seen by you before.

life list (n) the list of all the species you have seen.

lister (n) someone who keeps lists (life list, regional list, etc.). Not as bad as a 'ticker'.

lump (v, n) to combine species; the new species is termed a 'lump'. (*See* 'split'.)

megatick (n) a cosmic bird, normally a 'lifer', and generally something spectacular in its own right (not another cisticola!)

migrants (n) birds that undertake regular, seasonal movements. (*See* 'nomads'.)

near-endemic (adj) a species that is almost restricted to a specific country or habitat.

nomads (n) birds that move in an unpredictable fashion in response to local conditions (e.g. seed-eating birds in arid areas that follow rain). (*See* 'migrants' and 'irruption'.)

pelagic (adj, n) refers either to true seabirds (those that remain at sea except while breeding) or trips on boats in pursuit of these birds.

pishing (v) onomatopoeic; involves luring forest and bush birds into the open by making various noises by mouth or by sucking the back of the hand. (*See* 'squeaking'.)

split (v, n) species raised from subspecies to species level. The new species are termed 'splits'. (*See* 'lump'.)

squeaking (v) Like 'pishing' but typically higher pitched. More often used in the Americas, where birds respond better to higher-pitched sounds.

staked out (n) refers to rarities or other desirable species that are easy to 'twitch', i.e. they can be depended upon to appear at a particular site.

stringer (n) someone who often claims to have seen birds that are never seen by anyone else (probably derived from 'stringing you along'). Getting a reputation as a stringer is the kiss of death because no one will ever believe you.

stringy (adj) a doubtful sighting. (*See* 'stringer'.)

thrash (v) see 'flog'.

tick (n, v) a new bird. It means the same as 'lifer', but has a negative connotation, being reserved for very dull lifers or birds that were not seen well.

ticker (n) someone who watches birds primarily to add them to their 'life list'. This is derogatory – and deservedly so. My favourite ticker story is that of an American tourist who was busy working on his list while driving through the Karoo and didn't bother to look up at a Verreaux's Eagle because he'd seen one in Kenya 15 years before!

twitch (v) derived from literally shaking with excitement on seeing a good bird; now mostly taken to mean going to look for a rare bird that has been found by someone else. (*See* 'twitcher'.)

twitcher (n) someone who regularly chases after rare birds. Depending on your point of view it can be derogatory (because many twitchers seldom go looking for their own birds, and are interested only in seeing new species) or mildly complimentary (because it denotes a level of serious commitment to birding).

vagrant (n) a bird outside its normal range.

wants (n) birds that are on your 'hit list' for any given area or trip.

A twitcher twitching

BASIC EQUIPMENT

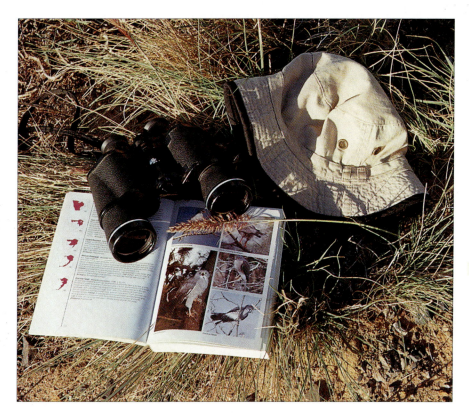

Like many male-dominated activities, birding can involve a lot of gadgets. But to start birding you really need only three items: binoculars, a field guide, a notebook. Of these, binoculars are the most important. Unfortunately, they are also the most problematic.

Choosing binoculars

Selecting the right pair of binoculars – 'bins' or 'noccies' – is a balance between cost and quality. A good pair can cost up to R12 000, but there are much cheaper models on the market, some of which are good enough to begin with. The important thing is to know what to look for when shopping.

The numbers game

Manufacturers delight in presenting statistics. The most important are the numbers presented in pairs, e.g. 8x30, 10x40, etc. The first figure gives the magnification (how many times larger the image appears); the second the width in millimetres of the objective lens (the light-gathering end of the binoculars).

Ideally, you want powerful bins (high magnification) with a large objective (for maximum light-gathering and a wide field of view). This, however, comes at a premium – large size and weight. You need to be able to carry your bins comfortably, even after a long day in the field. And unless you want to lug a tripod everywhere, you need to be able to hold them steady enough that the image doesn't bounce up and down – a problem that gets worse with increasing magnification and weight of the binoculars, as well as the age of the observer.

The result is a trade-off. As a rule, consider only binoculars with magnification 7–10x, and an objective lens width of 30–50 mm. Less than 7x is too weak; above 10x will not give you a steady image unless you stabilize your binoculars (by leaning against a tree, or resting your elbows on your knees or chest).

For forest work, where light is limited and birds are often close to the observer, 7–8x magnification serves well. It works well, also, for older and smaller people who have problems steadying the heavier 10x binoculars. In open habitats, where birds are often further away, 10x is better; 9x is an excellent compromise, but very few models are made with this magnification. Zoom binoculars that offer a range of magnifications may appear attractive, but they compromise on many other desirable features, and are best avoided.

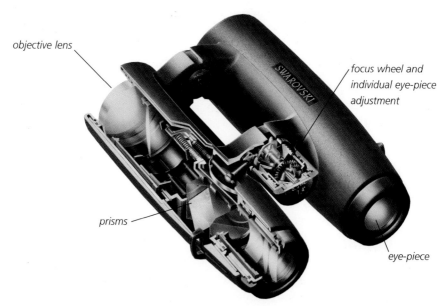

Modern roof-prism binoculars are lightweight, rugged and totally sealed against dust and moisture.

Another vital statistic is the close-focus distance. All binoculars focus from infinity to some minimum distance. For birding, especially in forests, you need to be able to focus to at least 3 m, and preferably closer. It's incredibly frustrating not to be able to focus on a bird because it's too close to you. Avoid 'focus free' binoculars – they work on the assumption that you want to look only at far-away objects and their close focus, hence, is worse than abysmal! Also, try to avoid 'rocker focus' devices; they lack the fine control of a focus wheel.

Some manufacturers quote the angle or field of view (given in degrees or feet at 1000 yards). Don't worry about this. As long as the width of the objective lens divided by the magnification is at least 4, you'll have a good field of view (but note this excludes most 'compact' binoculars). More important is the brightness and sharpness of the image. This depends in part on the quality of the optics and their coatings – and here you generally get what you pay for. Brightness also depends on the diameters of the objective lens and exit pupil (the circle of light visible in the eye-piece lenses when you look at them from a distance of 20–30 cm). The exit pupil should be at least 4–5 mm in diameter.

Beyond statistics

Assuming that the stats are OK, it is important to check other features of the model you are considering. How do the bins feel? Are they comfortable in your hand and round your neck? Are they too heavy? You can partially reduce the problem of heavy binoculars by using a broad, neoprene strap or a shoulder-support strap.

Do they have an adjustable eye-piece (normally the right one)? Is the field of view flat and crisp from edge to edge? Are the colours lifelike? A simple test is to focus on a thin, straight object (a phone line is ideal). If a coloured shadow image appears around the line (usually blue/yellow), there is chromatic aberration. If the line appears to bend towards the edge of the field of view, there is spherical aberration.

You also need to be happy that the bins will stand up to the rigours of birding. Are they robustly built? Is there a warranty? Are they waterproof? If the eye-pieces move in and out when you focus, they are probably not waterproof. A manufacturer's recommendation that you clean by rinsing under a tap is a good indication that they are!

Buyer's checklist for binoculars

Essential features for birding binoculars:
magnification: 7-10x, objective lens diameter 30-50 mm ✓
brightness/field of view: objective lens diameter ÷ magnification at least 4 ✓
close focus: at least 3-4 m, preferably closer ✓
image quality: sharp across the entire field of view; true-to-life colour (good lens coatings) ✓
weight: manageable for a long day in the field ✓
eye-pieces: individual eye-piece adjustment ✓

Nice to have features:

- waterproof, with fully internal focusing
- no spherical aberration (uniform magnification across the entire field of view)
- locking individual eye-piece adjustment
- retractable or fold-back eye-cups, especially if you wear glasses
- a rain guard that slips over the eye-pieces

Conventional, porro prism models **(1)** *have objectives that are wider than the eye-pieces. They are cheaper but generally heavier, less robust and are seldom waterproof. Roof prism models* **(2)** *are slimmer, lighter, tougher and are often totally sealed – all desirable traits. The only drawback is they tend to be more expensive. Compact binoculars* **(3)** *are scaled-down models with small objective lenses (under 30 mm). They're light and handy to take on hikes, but have a very limited field of view, making it difficult to locate and follow birds. They are not suitable for serious birding.*

Using binoculars

Binoculars are a tool, and to use them well requires practice. The first thing to do is to adjust them to your eyes (all decent binoculars have an adjustable eye-piece). Pick an object and focus on it using only your left eye and the central focusing wheel. Then focus the image for your right eye using the adjustable eye-piece. Both eyes should now have a crisp image of the object. At this point, you shouldn't need to touch the adjustable eye-piece again, and in a good pair of bins it can be locked so that it doesn't move accidentally.

Once you have your bins focused correctly, practise focusing on distant and close objects. You can't afford to waste time in the field turning the focus wheel the wrong way! An essential skill is locating birds (or other objects) in your field of view. Start with stationary objects. With your eyes on the target, slowly lift the binoculars to your eyes. You should find you're still looking at the target through the binoculars – but this requires practice. Once you've mastered this technique, try moving targets. The same principle applies. Track the bird with the naked eye and lift the bins to your eyes while tracking. The faster you can do this, the smaller the chance of losing the bird.

Caring for your bins

Good binoculars can last a lifetime, provided they are looked after. Keep them free of dirt and, especially, salt spray by washing under the tap (if waterproof). Clean the lenses only with lens tissue, a lens pen or soft cloth (an old, much-washed, cotton hanky is good). To avoid scratching the lens coating, blow dust and other particles off the lenses (preferably with a blower brush) before wiping them. But don't be shocked if you see people cleaning their lenses on their shirts – anything goes when you're in the field!

Locating a bird through binoculars takes practice, but soon becomes second nature.

Although tricky-sounding, this becomes second nature after a while and your binoculars begin to feel like an extension of your hands and eyes. Stabilize your bins, especially for prolonged use, by resting your elbows on your knees (sitting), chest (standing) or by leaning against a tree, rock or other large object. If there's a wind blowing, don't stand in an exposed position. For prolonged viewing of birds overhead (e.g. soaring raptors or forest canopy birds), try lying down. Just make sure that you're not lying on an ants' nest and that there are no lunch crumbs or other debris lurking in your eye cups that can end up in your eyes.

A WORD OF ADVICE
- *Keep your binocular straps short, so that you can lift them quickly to your eyes.*
- *Inverted binoculars make a handy magnifying glass for inspecting small things up close.*

A field guide

Once you've got your binoculars, and know how to use them, you're ready to start watching birds. At this stage, you'll need some assistance with bird identification.

Next to your bins, a field guide is your most important acquisition. The field guide format, pioneered by Roger Tory Peterson in the USA, concentrates on features that help to identify birds, and has the text conveniently situated opposite the illustrations. The format is generally small enough to fit into a large pocket and, literally, be used in the field.

Southern Africa is blessed with a plethora of excellent field guides and other bird books that make life easy for the beginner. This wasn't always the case – try to identify waders using the Norman Lighton plates in an old copy of *Roberts' Birds of Southern Africa* (pre-1978). And seabirds were even worse! The main problem a beginner has these days is choosing from the variety of books on offer.

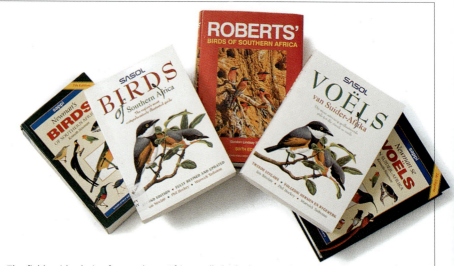

The field guide choice for southern Africa really boils down to Kenneth Newman's much-loved classic, Newman's Birds of Southern Africa, (7th ed., Struik) or the SASOL guide (SASOL Birds of Southern Africa by Ian Sinclair, Phil Hockey and Warwick Tarboton, 2nd ed., Struik). There are several photographic guides, but only Sinclair's Field Guide to the Birds of Southern Africa (2nd ed., Struik) is small enough to carry in the field.

Given the diversity of birds, photographs are not ideal to illustrate all the key identification features, let alone age- and sex-related variation. If you can afford to buy more than one book, a photographic guide is a useful supplement, especially for beginners who often find it easier to relate the birds they see to photographs than to illustrations. Sinclair and Davidson's large-format *Southern African birds: A Photographic Guide* (1st ed., Struik) is perhaps the best compromise between cost and photo selection.

PRACTICAL BIRDING

Both *Newman's* and *SASOL* are excellent field guides, well above the standard of guides for most other regions. Beginners often find *Newman's* easier to use because it is less detailed than *SASOL* and it tends to group similar-looking birds (e.g. swallows and swifts), even if they are not closely related. Most top birders prefer the SASOL guide's more comprehensive illustrations and more incisive text. See which suits you. If you become a serious birder, you'll probably end up with both. Beginners may find *Newman's Birds by Colour* (1st ed., Struik) useful, if only to get started.

The other book every southern African birder should be aware of is *Roberts' Birds of Southern Africa* (6th ed., John Voelcker Bird Book Fund by Gordon Maclean; the 7th ed. will be more of a handbook and is due for publication in 2004). Originally *the* bird book, *Roberts'* has largely been supplanted as an identification tool by recent field guides. However, it remains the best place to look if you want more information about birds. It gives detailed measurements, which are useful for identifying birds in the hand, and also describes habitats, behaviour, breeding biology and vocalizations.

And, if you can afford it, the *Atlas of Southern African Birds* (1997, BirdLife South Africa) is a fascinating, two-volume series that gives detailed information on bird distribution and movement patterns. Information on other useful books and resources is given in 'Guides and other books', pp. 91–92.

A notebook

The other basic tool for any self-respecting birder is a notebook. Many listers (someone who keeps lists) simply tick off the birds they see in their field guide, but real birders keep detailed notes of all their birding activities. Birders' notes are invaluable for identifying birds, and are an important source of scientific information. Detailed field descriptions are essential if you want to submit records of rare birds for evaluation (*see* p. 73).

Increasingly, people use computer data bases to store their records, and there are several packages custom-designed for the purpose, such as Thayer birding software (*see* 'Websites', p. 92). However, you still need to capture the information in the field, and for this there is little to compete with a handy, A6-sized notebook. Ideally, these should be waterproof, but, sadly, such notebooks are available in South Africa only as imports, and are fairly expensive.

If you do take notes in the rain, a pencil is best because it works on damp paper and the writing won't run if the notebook gets wet.

Some people prefer to use a small tape recorder to keep notes, because talking is generally quicker than writing. However, you can't sketch on a tape, and you need to transcribe the information at a later stage. You also run the risk of taping over something important.

BASIC EQUIPMENT

GETTING TO KNOW BIRDS 3

Long-tailed Widowbird

When you're just starting off as a birder, there are normally enough birds around to keep you busy. The problem is not so much finding birds as identifying them.

It is daunting to be faced with more than 900 possible species in a field guide to the birds of southern Africa. However, with patience (and a co-operative subject), virtually any bird can be identified by a process of elimination. Many of the birds in the book can be discarded because they are the wrong shape, size or colour, or don't occur in your area. Using this approach, you can narrow the options down to a few groups. From this point, identification of most species is straightforward, using the diagnostic characters highlighted in the field guide.

This section describes how to identify birds that you see and hear. It also points out some of the difficulties of bird identification resulting from variation within each species.

Making a field description

At the outset, the important thing is to train yourself to observe and memorize the features of any unknown bird. It helps if you can immediately place a bird to a specific group (for example, larks), but that's not essential as long as you capture the essential information.

Because memory is fallible, it's best to make a full description in your notebook before referring to the field guide. This forces you to really study all aspects of a bird, and stands you in good stead when you encounter a rarity or visit an area that lacks a convenient field guide.

A field description is a comprehensive description of all aspects of a bird, from its general size and shape, to a detailed account of its plumage and behaviour. A labelled sketch helps enormously to summarize the colouring and key plumage patterns.

Sketching and taking notes

In making a field description, you should note the following:

Habitat in which the bird is seen
macro-habitat: e.g. forest, grassland, desert, wetlands.
micro-habitat: e.g. ground or canopy, main trunks or outer branches.

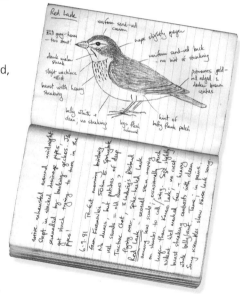

The bird
bill: How long is its bill relative to its head length? Is it straight or curved, slender or stout, hooked or not?
legs: How long are its legs? Do its feet extend beyond the tail in flight?
toes: How many toes does it have? How are they arranged? Are the toes webbed or lobed?
body shape: How long is its neck and tail? Do the folded wings extend beyond the tail? Is the tip of the tail rounded, squared, wedge-shaped or forked?
shape in flight: Are the wings short and rounded, long and slender, or some other shape? Do the primary feathers extend as separate fingers? Is the tail fanned or closed?
size: Best judged relative to adjacent birds. Failing that, compare size with that of well-known species such as sparrows or starlings. Be careful: it can be hard to estimate the size of a lone bird.
posture: Erect or horizontal? Is the neck extended or retracted (at rest and in flight)?

Activity and movement
foraging action: Does the bird hunt from a perch, glean from foliage or bark, dig in the ground, hammer wood, catch prey in the air, dive from the surface of the water, plunge-dive?
flight action: Level or undulating? Are flaps continuous or with interspersed glides? How rapid and deep are the wing beats (slow and deep versus fast and shallow)? How are the wings held (fully extended or bent at the wrist)?
gait: Does the bird walk or hop? How fast does it walk?
Once you have this information, it should be fairly easy to identify the type of bird, and then the species to which it belongs.

Natural versus artificial groupings

There are many ways of grouping birds. Most bird books, (e.g. *SASOL* and *Roberts*), list birds in a sequence that is thought to represent their evolutionary relationships, (see 'Classification and naming of birds', p. 27). This results in a 'natural' classifications i.e. one independent of human foibles, starting with ostriches and ending with canaries and buntings (but see the 'New classification of birds', p. 94). The advantage of this system is that it gives information about the relationships among birds, and is consistent throughout the world.

However, some distantly related birds can look very similar, because a bird's appearance results from its environment and lifestyle as well as its evolutionary history. *Newman's field guide* acknowledges this by grouping birds that look similar, or that occur in the same habitat. For example, swallows and swifts are not closely related, but they look similar as a result of their common lifestyle as aerial insectivores. This 'artificial' grouping is often rather forced. Newman's 'insect-eaters' include a diverse array of birds from larks to robins, some of which don't eat many insects!

SASOL field guide: *natural group*

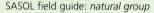
Thrushes, alethes, robins, chats, rockjumpers • Turdidae
W 314, A 121/96, S 45/15, S/A=37%
A highly diverse family; predominantly ground-dwelling. Thrushes, alethes and some robins are mostly forest species; some robin species are accomplished mimics. Chats inhabit open areas from deserts to savannas; less frequently in woodland. Rockjumpers, whose taxonomic affinities are unclear, inhabit montane grasslands and fynbos.

Newman's field guide: *artificial group*

Insect-eaters – Larks to Robins
This group of slender-billed insect-eating birds have similarities of shape and behaviour.

Newman's Birds by Colour takes the artificial classification system to its extreme by grouping birds by colour. This is fine for absolute beginners, but it is best to learn the natural groups as soon as possible, because learning birds solely by colour will not develop identification skills that you can take with you to other areas (where birds from the same natural groups may have very different colours).

Know the parts of a bird

In order to understand the key identification features in field guides and to be able to converse with other birders, you have to learn the various parts of a bird and the key plumage features. Most field guides have sketches depicting the main features, and two are reproduced here.

Again this may seem like a chore, but the names come quite easily once you start using them in field descriptions. First learn the names of the large, obvious features common to all birds (e.g. rump, vent, nape), then move on to more specialized features (e.g. distinguishing moustachial and malar stripes).

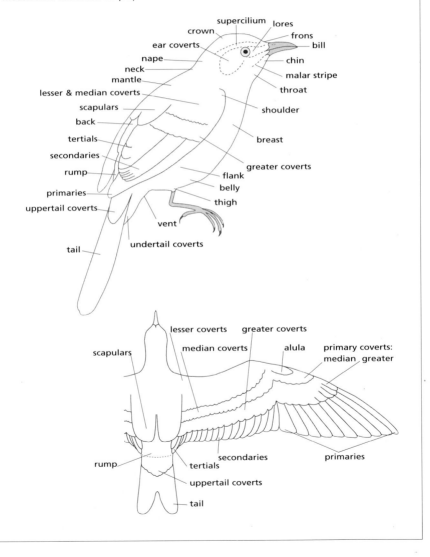

GETTING TO KNOW BIRDS

Recognizing bird groups

The key to successful bird identification is learning how to place an unknown bird into a group of similar species. The structure of a bird is most useful in identifying the general type of bird (bill shape, for instance, can tell you whether it is a bird of prey, a seed-eater or a nectar feeder); its colour and plumage pattern typically identify it to species.

Many beginners make the mistake of concentrating on a bird's colour and plumage pattern. These are important, but only after you know what sort of bird you're dealing with. Is it a waterbird, an insect-eating warbler or a bird of prey? The answer depends more on the size, shape, posture and behaviour of the bird than on its coloration.

If you want to be able to identify birds anywhere in the world, and communicate with other birders, you need to be familiar with the grouping of birds according to their evolutionary relationships. (See 'Natural versus artificial groupings', p.18). This might sound incredibly complicated, but is simply an extension of the instinctive recognition process whereby everyone 'knows' at least a few natural groups of birds – doves or ducks or pigeons or penguins.

Becoming familiar with the other groups is best achieved by identifying several species from each group in the field. The introductions to most field guides help by summarizing the main features of each grouping, but ultimately each birder has to develop a *gestalt* 'feel' for the group.

BILLS

Fruit eating e.g. Kurrichane Thrush

Nectar sipping e.g. Cape Sugarbird

Meat tearing e.g. Tawny Eagle

Filtering e.g. Greater Flamingo

Hammering e.g. Bearded Woodpecker

FEET

Floating e.g. Purple Gallinule

Wading e.g. Black-headed Heron

Clinging e.g. Olive Woodpecker

Perching e.g. Orange-breasted Rockjumper

Many types of birds can be distinguished by the shape of their bills and feet. Birds of prey have hooked bills for tearing flesh and strong, clawed talons for killing and holding prey. A bird with a long dagger-like bill and long legs, however, is likely to be a waterbird such as a heron or related species. But the differences between some groups (for instance robins and chats, both of which forage on the ground and eat insects) are subtle, and distinguishing between them is a challenge.

Identifying to species

Once you've identified the bird to the correct group (or one of a small subset of groups), it's usually fairly easy to identify it to species from the field guide. This is where coloration comes into play.

However, it's important to observe the pertinent aspects of a bird's coloration. It is very frustrating to spend a lot of time watching a bird and think you have all the features only to go to the field guide and discover that you needed to check the colour of the underwing coverts! For tricky groups, where there are several species that are superficially similar, it's a good idea to learn the differences in advance, so that you know exactly what to look for.

Ducks and doves are good groups on which to hone your identification skills. Left from top to bottom: *Cape Teal, Red-billed Teal* and *Yellow-billed duck*. Right from top to bottom: *African Mourning Dove, Cape Turtle Dove* and *Laughing Dove*.

If this sounds like hard work, don't despair. Start out with easy groups like doves or ducks. Both are easy to observe and have enough species to make it a bit of a challenge, but all the species have distinctive features that should make identification easy.

Once you are confident with one group, start to expand your horizons. Going out with someone knowledgeable can help, but all too often you end up being told everything. You tend to learn more when you struggle with identifications alone or with a fellow beginner. Leafing through photographs in glossy bird books and magazines also helps to test your fledgling skills, but there's nothing to compare with time spent in the field.

Plumage differences within a species

The identification of many species is complicated by differences in plumage with age, sex or season, or between birds of the same species in different regions. Sometimes these differences can be useful (for instance, they allow studies of age- or sex-related differences in behaviour), but for the beginner they may be confusing.

Differences in plumage with age

Some birds leave the nest in 'adult' plumage, but others have distinct, age-related plumages. Many birds have a juvenile plumage which is retained until the first moult, when adult plumage is attained. For example, many passerines (perching songbirds) have a distinctive juvenile plumage that lasts only a few weeks after leaving the nest. If you come across one of these birds without its parents, you might begin to believe you've found a new species!

Juvenile plumages are seldom illustrated in field guides. Useful indicators are very new, fresh feathers, often with buff fringes or spotting. In passerines, juveniles also have sharply pointed tail feathers, whereas those of adults have broader tips. Size is not useful, because most birds reach adult size in all dimensions (except for subtle differences in bill size) shortly after fledging.

Adult (left) and juvenile Kurrichane Thrush. Many young passerines are spotted below, but this plumage only lasts a few weeks. The sharply pointed tail feathers last longer.

Other birds have three age-related plumages: juvenile, immature (which may be retained for one or more years), and adult. Some large birds make a birder's life even more difficult by having three or more distinct plumages before acquiring adult plumage (e.g. some albatrosses, eagles and large gulls). This is taken to its extreme by Wandering Albatrosses, which gradually become paler over twenty or more years. In these birds, you can refer to the plumage by the age of the bird (e.g. a Kelp Gull in third year plumage).

For some tricky groups, e.g. waders and raptors, knowledge of the age/sex of the bird you're looking at is particularly important. The details of within-species plumage variation are summarized in good field guides, but not all plumages are illustrated.

Birds in active moult can also be confusing, because they have a mix of plumages or have gaps in their plumage that reveal unexpected patterns. A common example is for pale patches to appear in otherwise dark upperwings during moult, when the pale bases of underlying feathers are exposed (e.g. Kelp Gull).

Many non-passerines have complex, age-related plumages. Antarctic Tern breeding adult (top), immature (centre) and juvenile (bottom).

There are more subtle age-related differences. Melanin, the main pigment that makes feathers dark, also strengthens feathers, making them more resistant to wear. Consequently, birds with old feathers lose some characteristics such as pale notches on individual feathers, or pale terminal bars to the wing or tail. They also often appear browner than birds in fresh plumage.

Differences in plumage with sex and season

Variations in plumage with sex and season are more straightforward.

Most birds that show sexual dimorphism (distinct male and female plumages) only do so when they acquire adult plumage. In general, males are more colourful and distinctive whereas females tend to be drabber and usually resemble immature birds. There are exceptions, however, especially in species where males carry the burden of chick rearing alone (e.g. phalaropes and painted snipes). Species with extreme plumage dimorphism tend to have polygamous mating systems, where one male mates with many females (e.g. Long-tailed Widowbird).

Seasonal plumage differences tend to be linked to breeding activity, with one plumage (differentiated by sex) for the breeding season, and a more camouflaged, non-breeding plumage for the rest of the year.

Red Bishops are highly sexually dimorphic, but the male (left) only has his bright plumage in the breeding season. For the rest of the year he resembles the female (right).

24 Differences in plumage with region

To complicate matters further, the appearance of some species varies between regions. This variation is described formally as a series of subspecies. In most cases, it involves only subtle changes in size or coloration, but in some species (e.g. many larks and some francolins) the regional variation is comparable to, or may even exceed, differences between species. Fortunately, the better field guides illustrate many of the extreme geographical variants.

Some species vary in colour between different parts of their range. Spike-heeled Larks in northern Namibia (right) are much paler than southern birds (left).

PRACTICAL BIRDING

Geographic variation may be gradual (termed 'clinal' variation) or may occur over a short distance ('stepped clines'). Where the variants are isolated from the rest of the population ('disjunct' populations), there is often debate as to whether the isolates should be regarded as distinct species. Even where ranges are continuous, investigation of some stepped clines indicates that two or more species are involved, with narrow hybrid zones between them.

It is best to be aware of major geographical variants and to keep track of which forms you see. If their status changes, you may have an informed opinion to air to your fellow birders and, at least, the luxury of an 'armchair tick'!

Colour morphs and other oddities

Another source of variation is the presence of different colour varieties or 'morphs' within a population. This typically involves pale and dark morphs, although intermediates often occur too. Colour morphs are common amongst raptors, and also occur among seabirds (skuas and some petrels and boobies) and a few other bird groups and species (e.g. egrets, Red-billed Quelea).

Most polymorphic species are predatory. One theory is that rare colour morphs have an advantage because prey species are less likely to recognize them as a threat, resulting in an increase in their numbers over time until another form becomes favoured. This is an example of what is termed an evolutionarily stable system.

Finally, there are rare plumage variants that result from mutations or are carried at low levels in the population on recessive genes (i.e. genes that are expressed only when they are represented on both maternal and paternal chromosomes). These confer no advantage, and occur purely by chance and in very small numbers (see Coloration abnormalities, p. 71).

Beyond plumage – jizz

Beyond plumage and basic structure, there is a suite of subtle shape, posture and behaviour characters that helps to differentiate similar species. Collectively these constitute a bird's jizz, a term attributed to the Second World War concept of 'General Impression of Size and Shape' used in the training of aircraft spotters to differentiate enemy planes from friendly forces.

Without a size reference, a Marsh Sandpiper (left) superficially resembles the larger Greenshank (right), but is more delicately built, with a much more slender bill.

When you first start, you might be forgiven for thinking that jizz is part of the system to keep beginners in their place. But differences in jizz really do exist, and can be tremendously important. Jizz is especially helpful in identifying groups such as some warblers, where there are very few other distinctive characters to separate the species (e.g. reed warblers). It is also valuable when you only get a distant, brief view of a bird, as in many seabird sightings. A difference in jizz can also be useful for detecting rare birds amongst a horde of common species, as in wader flocks or the vast seabird aggregations that gather behind trawlers.

There's no easy way to get a feel for jizz – it's more an art form than a science, and comes with experience in the field. It is defined almost exclusively in relative terms. Thus you might hear that such dissimilar species as Kerguelen Petrels and Barlow's Larks both appear bull-necked, but this is relative to Great-winged Petrels and Karoo Larks, respectively. You can say you've finally arrived as a birder once you can hold your own in discussions about the jizz of various birds.

Birding by ear

Although they communicate visually for the most part, birds also make extensive use of sound. Most species have distinctive songs and other calls by which you can identify them without having seen them. Indeed, many skulking species such as rails, flufftails and some warblers are much more often heard than seen.

Some birds are easily overlooked if they aren't calling.

Classification and naming of birds

Taxonomy, the science of classifying organisms, strives to group closely related species in a nested hierarchy of genera (groups of closely related species), families (groups of related genera) and orders (groups of related families). This classification system attempts to summarize the evolutionary relationships among birds. Thus species in the same genus are believed to be more closely-related than are species from different genera. One consequence of using a natural classification system is that the arrangement changes as new information becomes available. (*See* the new proposed sequence at the back of this book.)

At the highest level, all birds are grouped together in the Class Aves, and differ from all other organisms by having feathers. Within Aves, many categories are recognized, but the most frequently used are orders (names ending in -iformes), families (-idae), subfamilies (-inae), genera and species. Each bird species, like all living organisms, has a unique scientific name. This is in two parts: the first is the genus, while the second identifies the species. This second, specific name always starts with a lower case letter, whereas all other levels are capitalized. The genus and species names are always italicized, but family and higher levels are not.

If we compare four species:

	Class	Order	Family	Genus	Species
Black Eagle	Aves	Falconiiformes	Accipitridae	*Aquila*	*verreauxii*
Pied Crow	Aves	Passeriformes	Corvidae	*Corvus*	*albus*
Cape Wagtail	Aves	Passeriformes	Motacillidae	*Motacilla*	*capensis*
Cape Longclaw	Aves	Passeriformes	Motacillidae	*Macronyx*	*capensis*

All are birds (Aves), but the eagle is in a different order from the crow, wagtail and longclaw (which are all passerines, the largest order of birds). The wagtail and longclaw are in the same family but in different genera. Thus the wagtail and longclaw are thought to be more closely related to each other than to the eagle or crow. But the crow is closer to both than the eagle, because it shares the same order. Note that species from different genera can have the same species name (at least 20 African birds are called *capensis*, literally 'of the Cape').

Unlike scientific names, where rigorous rules prevent name clashes, the same common name is often used for more than one species (e.g. there are different 'Black' Eagles in Africa and Asia) or there is more than one name for the same species (e.g. Cape and Orange-throated Longclaw are both commonly used for *Macronyx capensis*). Southern Africa has tended to use different common names from those used elsewhere for many of its birds.

The International Ornithological Committee recently produced a standard list of common English names for the world's birds (the African Black Eagle, for instance, is called Verreaux's Eagle, the species' common name in East Africa). Some local names are likely to persist through habit, but the standard names will, hopefully, prevail. It makes the life of the travelling birder much easier if there aren't regional ambiguities and clashes in common names.

For some groups such as cisticolas and pipits, the song is the main diagnostic feature of many species. I doubt there are many birders who can confidently separate Cloud from Ayres' Cisticola without hearing them call. Bird calls are also important aids to locating birds, especially in dense, cluttered habitats such as forests, thickets and reed beds. Birds in these habitats tend to make more use of song than birds in more open environments, because sound is more effective than visual displays for signalling.

Knowing the calls of the common species in an area is an enormous advantage. You don't waste time tracking down the calls of what turns out to be a common bird. You can also compile area lists efficiently for 'atlasing' purposes (see p. 81) and compete more successfully in events such as big day competitions (see p. 65).

But how can you learn the myriad bird calls? Word descriptions of bird calls are notoriously subjective, which reduces the value of descriptions in field guides. Obviously, the best way is to spend a lot of time in the field, studying all the birds and the calls they make – a luxury few can afford. However, the learning process can be supplemented by using recordings.

The main drawback to commercial recordings is that they often present only the main song of each species. Also, they seldom present the range of regional variation in song. Just as there is racial variation in plumage, so song dialects also vary geographically.

Another problem with using song to identify birds is that you have to be alert for mimicry. Several species incorporate elements of other species' songs in their repertoire, and some species are such good mimics that they can confuse even experienced birders. In South Africa, the robin-chats are perhaps the most proficient and best-known mimics, but many other species also mimic, including some larks, chats and drongos. Introduced Indian Mynas and European Starlings are also excellent mimics.

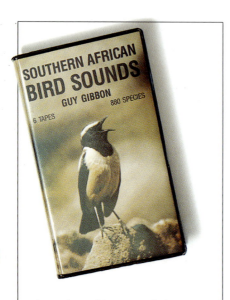

In southern Africa, we are lucky to have an almost complete set of bird calls available commercially. Guy Gibbon's Southern African Bird Sounds on cassette tape or CD is the most comprehensive product, and these calls are used on the CD ROM version of Roberts' Birds of Southern Africa in a fun quiz. The complete set of Gibbon's tapes can be cumbersome to use in the field, but there are some handy compilations of frequently used calls such as Gibbon's LBJ tape, which brings together the songs of warblers, cisticolas, larks, pipits and other nondescript 'little brown jobs' on a single cassette.

Learning to sing

Birds differ in their ability to learn different songs. Some birds have inherent songs hard-wired into them. Even if reared in isolation, they sing the 'correct' song. This is the case for most non-passerines (all birds other than the large order Passeriformes), the sub-oscine passerines (pittas and broadbills are the only sub-oscines in Africa), as well as brood parasites (birds that lay their eggs in the nests of other birds, such as cuckoos). These species typically have rather simple songs, with little regional variation.

The ability to learn songs is confined to parrots, hummingbirds and oscine passerines (the vast majority of African songbirds). Indeed, it has been argued that the large number of passerine species evolved partly because learning songs facilitates reproductive isolation. Typically, only the main advertising or territorial song is learned; contact calls and alarm calls are innate (i.e. genetically programmed).

Most species that learn 'their' song by listening to their parents and other members of the same species have an innate template that determines the basic structure of the song. This prevents them from inadvertently learning songs of the wrong species. Relatively few species are good mimics that incorporate sounds from their environment, including other species' songs, into their repertoire. It has been shown that in at least some of these species, females select males based on their vocal acuity, encouraging the development of the ability to mimic.

For most species, there is a critical period of a few months when a young bird learns its song. Even parrots, renowned for their ability to mimic human phrases, seldom add to their repertoire after they are two years old. Relatively few species continue to learn and improvise throughout their lives.

A Cape Longclaw (above) and Bokmakierie (right), both in full song

Sonograms: visualising song

In the absence of recordings of birdsongs, sonograms offer a more objective method of description than do words. Sonograms also help you to detect the subtle differences between similar birdsongs. For example, Karoo and Barlow's larks have songs that sound rather similar, but by studying their sonograms you can train your ear to detect the differences.

Sonograms represent bird calls visually by plotting call intensity (energy) as a function of pitch (frequency) and time. Time is plotted on the horizontal axis, and pitch on the vertical axis, with high-pitched notes appearing higher up than low-pitched notes. This is best illustrated through some well-known examples.

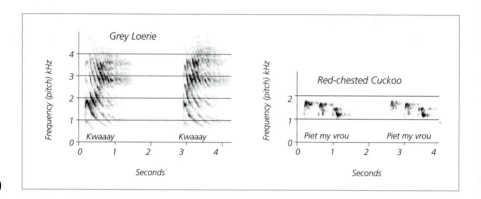

You can also get an idea of the tonal quality of a call by looking at the structure of the energy distribution. Clear, whistled notes, such as those of robin-chats or thrushes, tend to have a single, well-defined structure whereas harsh calls, like those of the Grey Loerie or Go-away bird, are much more diffuse. Matching bands of energy denote harmonics, and imply a richer tone than simple whistles.

Making your own sonograms

With the advent of personal computers, any birder can make a sonogram from his or her own recordings, commercial tape or from recordings obtained from sound libraries. The software package of choice is Canary, produced by the Cornell Laboratory of Ornithology (www.ornith.cornell.edu/BRP/), but this runs only on Apple computers. For the majority of 'deprived' South Africans who use IBM clone PCs, the website has links to a suite of PC-based packages. Avi-soft and Cool Edit are satisfactory. (See p. 77 for more information on making recordings and on sound libraries.)

FIELD SKILLS 4

Once you've learned the basic skills of bird identification, it's time to venture further afield in search of birds in different environments and habitats. Successful birding requires a range of field skills depending on the habitat and the type of bird that is sought.

This section describes the different approaches you need when birding from a vehicle, on foot, at night and at sea. It also describes how to use tapes to locate birds on land – and a couple of alternative approaches to locating birds.

Birding from a vehicle

Vehicles make great mobile hides, often allowing you to get closer to birds than you could on foot. They also enable you to cover large distances and thus to encounter more birds, especially large, wide-ranging birds such as raptors (birds of prey), cranes and bustards. Consequently, much birding is done from cars, especially in open habitats.

Here are some pointers to boost your success.

- **Choose the best route.** Don't try to bird from a busy road. Apart from inconveniencing other motorists, you are less likely to see birds. It's very annoying, moreover, to have an interesting bird chased off by a passing car. Choose a route that takes you through a range of habitats. More raptors are found on roads with telephone poles than on those without these handy perches. If you're venturing into a new area, check bird-finding guides (listed in the final section of this book) for suggested routes.
- **Orient yourself for light.** Try to drive with your back to the sun for the best light – west in the morning and east in the afternoon (which is tricky if you live on the west coast!).
- **Drive slowly.** This allows you more time to look for birds and also to look at each bird and assess whether it's worth stopping for. If you do see something that warrants investigation, you will be able to stop more quickly and, at lower speeds, you are less likely to flush the bird.
- **Don't stop right next to birds.** Birds are more likely to flush if you stop right next to them. If you can't stop before you reach a bird perched next to the road, roll on past, gently slowing down, and then look back at the bird. Have at least one person keep an eye fixed on the bird in case it flushes anyway.
- **Keep the windows open.** This lets you hear bird calls, which are important when locating certain birds (see 'Birding by ear', p. 26).
- **Stop, scan and listen.** Stopping every so often allows you to hear better and also to scan surrounding areas with binoculars. Birds such as bustards and coursers often avoid the area close to the road but can be detected with binoculars. Stop at places with a good vantage or at sites such as wetlands, river bridges and road cuttings.
- **Choose the best time of day.** Birds are most active in the early morning and, to a lesser extent, evening. Also, many birds commute to and from roost sites at these times. Consequently, these are the best times for road birding.
- **Drive safely.** Car-based birding works best when there are several spotters and a dedicated driver. Don't stop in dangerous places and, when you stop, pull the car off the road. Notwithstanding these admonitions, don't be surprised if you come across a car slewed across the road with all four doors wide open – just look for the birders. Some bird clubs sell bumper stickers that warn other drivers: 'Birdwatcher: beware of sudden stops'.

Birding on foot

Although many birders seem welded to their car seats, at least some foot slogging is needed to get to grips with most bird species. To improve your chances of finding birds and getting a good enough look to be able to identify them, there are several things to keep in mind:

- **Look for movement.** Movement is the single most important clue to a bird's position. Train your eye to detect the slightest movement within dense foliage; this is how top birders detect so many more birds than beginners. It is easier to detect movement on still days, but even when it's windy, look for things moving the 'wrong' way in wind-blown foliage. Birding in the rain is even trickier; the dripping of water onto leaves is unpredictable, and the resultant movement is like that of a bird.
- **Decide on the balance between walking and waiting.** Birds are very quick to detect your movements. You get longer, more intimate views if you sit quietly until the birds forget your presence. But you can also spend a lot of time sitting and seeing nothing at all. Whether to walk or wait depends in part on the type of habitat in which you're birding. In open habitats, you have a good chance of seeing any bird that you disturb and, generally, you can relocate the bird by watching where it lands. Approaching cautiously should then result in a good view of the bird. In forests, on the other hand, birds can easily slip away without being seen, so you have to use more guile. Here, sitting and waiting is often more rewarding.

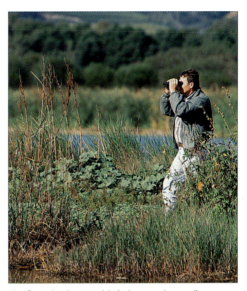

On foot, it's best to bird alone or in small groups.

- **Select the right spot.** You can boost your chances by birding favourable sites. If you're waiting for birds to appear, find a site where your body is hidden from view, but where you have a good vantage over a range of micro-habitats (forest floor, mid-strata, canopy). Although avoided by some species, the fringes of habitats are more diverse. It also pays to wait near a feature that attracts birds, such as water, a fruiting tree, or a driver ant swarm (don't get too close!). The one drawback to waiting near a stream is that its noise tends to mask bird calls.
- **Don't bird in large groups.** The waiting strategy depends on remaining still and quiet, and is probably most successful for no more than one or two birders sitting together. If you must bird in a group, pick your partners with care – leave the garrulous ones at home.

- **Move at the right pace.** Most birding on foot entails moving slowly and quietly through the habitat, looking and listening for birds. Once you locate something of interest, move towards it as calmly and cautiously as possible, looking for any movement that betrays the bird's position.
- **Orient yourself for light.** Irrespective of whether you're waiting or walking, always try to put your back to the sun, so that the best possible light falls on any birds you see.
- **Listen for bird calls and other sounds.** Bird calls are a good indication of where to look for birds. Alarm calls (or sudden crouching or flushing) may indicate a raptor overhead. The presence of a bird is betrayed not only by songs and calls, however. Listen for woodpeckers and other birds tapping, or the sound of wings flapping (especially on take off), feet scrabbling on bark, the rain of seeds caused by messy feeders, or the rustle of birds walking on or raking over dried leaves.
- **Wear the right clothes.** If you want to watch birds doing their thing rather than fleeing for the horizon, wear something that blends with the background and isn't too noisy. Ditch the shocking pink T-shirt and windbreaker that rustles every time you walk. In general, dark clothing is better.

Marsh bashing

The one exception to birding in small groups and moving quietly is when you're trying to flush crakes, quails and other skulking species that live in tall grasslands or shallow marshes. Here you want as many people making as much noise as possible! Walk line abreast, about 5–10 m apart, and systematically quarter the area. Don't just tramp along at a fixed pace; stop occasionally, and meander around. Many skulkers crouch and freeze when they hear you approach, and are less likely to flush if you move predictably. Shouting and clapping may help.

Marsh bashing does not give you quality views; birds pop up unexpectedly, fly directly away from the line, then crash back into the dense vegetation. You need to be ready at all times (bins in hand) and make sure everyone shouts whenever something flushes. As a selfish birder, it's probably best to be in the middle of the line to maximize your chance of getting a decent view of any fleeing bird.

Marsh bashing is controversial because of the impact on the vegetation and the animals. The severity of this impact depends on how often it occurs. Bashing through a marsh in the middle of nowhere is unlikely to do much damage, but more restraint is required in well-birded areas and nature reserves. A better option is to use a well-trained gamebird dog to locate and flush birds. And you're less likely to dip, because you know where the birds are going to flush.

PRACTICAL BIRDING

Using recordings

Many birds respond to playback of their song, or even to a whistled imitation. This is an excellent way to locate specific birds (especially at night) and to lure skulking species out of dense vegetation. To use tapes, all you need is a tape player and a recording of the target bird's song. Be careful; excessive playing of tapes can disturb birds. Some birders frown on the use of tapes, preferring to use their own skills and patience to locate birds.

Using commercial tapes is not always effective, particularly at stakeouts (where many birders go in pursuit of a particular bird), because the bird has heard the commercial tape too often and no longer bothers responding. Recording and playing back a bird's own song (see 'Making recordings', p. 77) is often more successful.

A few words of advice when playing back bird calls:

- **Don't play tapes continuously.** To locate a particular species, play the tape at intervals of 50–100 m as you traverse suitable habitat, until you get a response. Continuous play may intimidate local territory holders.
- **Wait a few minutes after playing the tape.** Birds often take some time to respond. Keep your eyes peeled for territory holders who often come to investigate the intruder without responding vocally.
- **Don't play tapes too loudly.** Loud calls can intimidate birds. Tape volume should not exceed the volume of the bird's own singing, or you may stimulate birds too far away from you to hear them!
- **When you get a response, use the bird's song to locate the bird.** If the bird stops calling, you can try using the tape again, but don't play the tape continuously as this might well frighten away the bird.
- **Remain quiet and still.** If you want to call a bird out of dense vegetation, be as unobtrusive as possible. Preferably hide yourself from the bird's view.
- **Use remote playback.** You can protect very shy species from the sight of you by playing their calls through a remote speaker, or leaving the tape recorder on at some distance from you (using either a loop tape or pre-recording of the specific song on a cassette).
- **Calling up owls.** Tapes are very useful for night birding. If you want to play a number of owl calls at a single site, start with the smallest species first because they are often scared off by larger owls (which are not averse to eating the smaller species!).
- **Try using your own recordings.** Commercial tapes are often ineffective because they have a different dialect, or because the bird has heard the commercial tape too often and no longer bothers responding. The problem of habituation typically occurs at stakeouts, where many birders go in pursuit of a specific bird. Playing back a bird's own song often evokes the strongest response.

Managing tapes

Gibbon's Southern African Bird Sounds is very comprehensive, but you're likely to need recordings of only a subset of species. You can waste a lot of time scrolling through tapes looking for the recordings you need, especially if you keep needing two calls on the same cassette. Consequently, it helps to make up customized cassettes for each habitat or location. Using CDs improves access time, but Gibbon's CD set, unfortunately, stores 10 bird species per track. The new DAT and mini-disc technologies offer the best solution, with vast storage space, virtually instant access, and automatic track repeat functions.

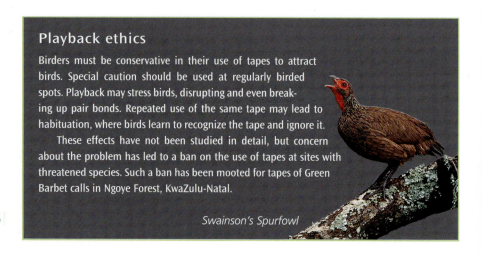

Playback ethics

Birders must be conservative in their use of tapes to attract birds. Special caution should be used at regularly birded spots. Playback may stress birds, disrupting and even breaking up pair bonds. Repeated use of the same tape may lead to habituation, where birds learn to recognize the tape and ignore it.

These effects have not been studied in detail, but concern about the problem has led to a ban on the use of tapes at sites with threatened species. Such a ban has been mooted for tapes of Green Barbet calls in Ngoye Forest, KwaZulu-Natal.

Swainson's Spurfowl

Other ways of attracting birds

The most common way, by far, to locate birds or lure them out of hiding is to mimic or play back their calls. Other techniques, however, can be effective, and site selection is important. These techniques work best if you're in an area where there are lots of birds, and if you are screened from the birds by a hide or by vegetation.

- **Pishing and squeaking.** Many bush birds are attracted by various pishing noises, which are thought to resemble a generalized alarm call, prompting birds to come out and mob a predator such as a snake or owl. Pishing and squeaking tend to work best in the breeding season. Some birds appear to respond best to a sibilant ksssh kssshing. Others favour higher-pitched psssing or psshing, made by sucking the back of your hand. In the Americas, higher-pitched squeaking works best, and many birders carry a 'squeaker' which produces high-pitched squeaks when twisted. The main drawback to using your hand or a squeaker is that it is difficult to hold your binoculars steady at the same time.
- **Imitating predators.** Another very useful technique in some habitats is to imitate the call of a predator that is routinely mobbed by small birds. The best known example in southern Africa is the call of the Pearl-spotted Owlet. In savanna areas, this can rapidly attract a large number of birds of many species. It can also call up an owlet!

- **Using models.** Visual lures are less often used than vocal ones, but they are also effective. Putting out the replica of an owl while imitating its call can get a good response from bush birds. Presenting a bird with a potential competitor (another male) can also be used to lure a particularly recalcitrant customer such as a flufftail into the open. Be sensitive, however, to the disturbance this might cause the bird.
- **Providing food.** This topic is covered in more detail in the section on garden birds (see p. 44), but food can be used as a lure anywhere, and can be especially useful at sea. One birder so successfully habituated a pair of Red-chested Flufftails by regular feeding that he had merely to splash in the muddy feeding area and they came running.

Birding in national parks

When birding in many African national parks, you are forced to remain in your car most of the time. This means that you can't pursue birds that offer a tantalizing glimpse as they flit over the road or are calling away from the road. Some birders flout the regulations, but this can put a premature end to a birding career. In one infamous case, a bird-tour guide went round a bush in India to check out a bird and was killed by a tiger!

Ideally you want a vehicle that is high enough to let you see over the tall grass that grows along road verges (as a result of the extra rain that runs off the road). Don't spend all your time driving; wait a while if you are watching for birds in dense habitats, and using tapes to lure birds out of hiding or other methods such as pishing and hissing (see 'Other ways of attracting birds', p. 36). If you have a telescope it is important to use a window mount or bean bag to make it easy to use the 'scope in the car (a bean bag will come in handy for a camera too). Spend a fair amount of time birding at camp sites and picnic sites where you are allowed out of the car.

Another problem is that many parks restrict driving at night. Some night birding can be done at camp sites, but it's a good idea to chat to the park staff about organizing a bird-oriented night drive.

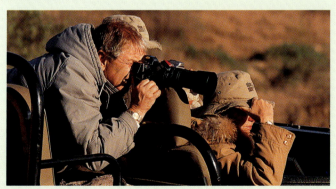

Even open vehicles serve as mobile hides.

Night birding

Nightjars, most owls and some coursers are active mainly at night. You might bump into them during the day while they're roosting, but the best way to see them is to go out at night. This requires a little more equipment than birding during the day, but the basic approaches are the same:

- Drive around scanning with a spotlight.
- Follow bird calls.
- Play calls and lure the birds to you.

One of the attractions of night birding is that you're likely to see mammals (such as bushbabies) seldom encountered during the day.

The main piece of equipment needed for night birding is a strong light. A bright and robust torch is adequate for most night birding on foot. It should have a beam that can be focused, and it should be water resistant and not too heavy on batteries (a Maglight or clone is pretty reliable).

IS IT HARMFUL?
It is often asked whether bright spotlights damage the eyes of nocturnal birds. The answer appears to be a qualified 'No'. Until their eyes readjust to the dark, however, the birds' hunting ability may be impaired.

For night drives, a halogen spotlight is preferable as torches lack sufficient power to locate distant birds. This should be from 0.5–1 million candlepower, and can be purchased from motor spares shops or outdoor recreation stores. They run off 12-volt DC, and usually come with an adapter to plug into a car cigarette lighter. This is fine while you are in the car, but limits mobility away from the vehicle. A neat solution is to buy a small, sealed-cell 12-volt battery (mass about 2 kg) that can be carried in a sling and runs the spotlight for about an hour before it needs recharging. It is available from specialist battery suppliers or from up-market camping outlets. A trickle-charger (available from motor spares shops) will recharge the battery overnight if you have access to an AC outlet. Failing that, a small solar panel will do the job.

Warm, still evenings are the best time to look for night birds. Owls that rely on sound to hunt prefer calm conditions, and the level of activity of most nocturnal birds peaks after dusk and before dawn. Nightjars often rest on roads, especially in the evening. While night driving, look for eye shine; most nocturnal creatures (including some spiders) have a reflective layer at the back of their eyes to make maximal use of the limited light available. With practice, you can tell birds' eyes from those of less interesting animals such as sheep.

Night birding equipment checklist	
torch: water resistant with a bright, focused beam	✓
spotlight: preferably 0.5–1 million candle-power. Separate 12-V battery and recharger	✓
spare bulbs for torch/spotlight	✓
tape player and tapes	✓
warm clothing for night drives – even in the tropics!	✓
a glove for the hand holding the spotlight	✓

Seabirding

True seabirds – those that come ashore only to breed – offer some of the most challenging and frustrating birding. The oceanic environment off southern Africa is one of the most dynamic and diverse marine environments in the world. To the south lies the Southern Ocean, a seabird mecca that provides superb sea birding off Africa's southern shores. Almost half of all the world's seabirds have been recorded within 200 nautical miles of southern Africa, compared with the region's recorded total of about 10 per cent of the world's land birds. Owing to the lack of breeding islands, however, most seabirds are non-breeding visitors, and many are rare or occur only as vagrants.

Birders love a challenge, and seabirds consequently attract a disproportionate amount of attention. There is more to seabirding, however, than physical hardship and the adrenaline rush of seeing a rare species. Some seabirds, such as the great albatrosses, are among the most majestic of birds and seeing them is well worth the effort involved.

You may adopt one of two approaches to seabirding:

Sea watching

As the name suggests, this often means watching a lot more sea than birds! Choose a suitable vantage point – preferably a promontory such as a pier or headland – and sit with your eyes glued to your binoculars or, preferably, telescope for long hours waiting for the occasional seabird to fly past. Given that most truly pelagic seabirds tend to stay well off the shore, this works best in foul weather when there are strong onshore winds. It's often cold and wet, and most of the birds are too far away to identify even with a 'scope, but occasionally it reaps rewards. It can also be a lot of fun in groups.

The following is a typical sea-watching exchange:
'*Southern Fulmar going right.*'
'*Where?*'
'*Just gone behind that big wave.*'
'*The one with the three gannets over it?*'
'*No, two cormorants.*'
'*Is it near the tanker?*'
'*I can't see any ships, but I've lost it now...*'

The secret to successful sea watching is to select the right spot and to be patient. Seabirds react to water depth, so you're better off at a headland where the continental shelf is narrow, for instance the Cape Peninsula or the east coast north of Port Alfred. But anywhere can be good at times. Mike Fraser accumulated an impressive list from his lounge window in Glencairn.

Another trick is to know when to bother looking. The wind should be directly on shore, not cross shore. Thus, Kommetjie, one of the best sea-watching sites in the Cape, works well in a north-westerly wind, whereas the Cape of Good Hope is good when the wind is from the south-west. Extreme weather also helps – watch the weather forecasts for cyclone warnings!

Finally, time of day is important. Seabirds are often closer to shore in the early morning (but weigh this against bad light if you're looking east).

Going to sea

Sea watching may whet your appetite, but going to sea is really the only way to satisfy your seabirding needs. It gets you right up to the birds, but requires access to an ocean-going boat, which isn't easy or cheap.

Fortunately, there are regular pelagic birding trips arranged out of Cape Town (all year) and Durban

TIPS ON SURVIVING SEASICKNESS

• *Stay on deck and look at the horizon.*
• *Eat something to settle your stomach.*
• *Avoid areas with engine fumes.*
• *Stand near the centre of the ship where movement is least.*
• *If you're feeling nauseous, throwing up can make you feel better.*
• *If you remain nauseous, find a dry, safe place to lie down.*

Birders enjoying the pelagic seabird spectacle

PRACTICAL BIRDING

(mostly in winter) where you can pool resources with other birders and have experts aboard to help identify some of the confusing species. Less regular trips are also being tried out of other centres (East London, Port Elizabeth, Plettenberg Bay). Check with the local bird clubs for details (see 'SA Bird Clubs', p. 90).

The main drawback is that boat trips tend to be on small vessels and conditions aboard are often unpleasant. Spending eight hours heaving over the gunwale while being showered in cold sea spray has to rate as one of life's least enjoyable experiences. Even if you don't get sick (and everyone should take anti-nausea pills before sailing!), just hanging on to a bucking ship for that length of time is pretty tiring.

OTHER TIPS
- *Keep cameras and any other electronic equipment well protected from salt spray.*
- *If your binoculars get coated in salt, lick the lenses before wiping them – salt crystals scratch!*
- *'Chumming' (throwing fish and/or fish oil overboard) often attracts seabirds to you.*

Not that this should put you off. Getting in behind a trawler with 5 000 albatrosses and petrels all around you rates as one of southern Africa's greatest birding experiences.

One of the challenges of going to sea on a specialist seabirding trip is to see the birds that everyone else sees. This might sound trite, but it's not a trivial problem. The rarer species often flit past the boat once, and you've got to get on to them first time. Most trips will have experienced leaders who are likely to spot most of the good birds first. Try to stand near the leaders and make sure you understand their reference system (practise on common birds so you don't learn the hard way that you aren't on the same wave length). Most guides use a clock system, with the bow as 12 o'clock, the stern 6 o'clock, port beam as 9 o'clock, etc. A typical instruction might be 'Leach's Petrel, 50 m at 2 o'clock, going away' (i.e. 50 m from the boat, slightly forward of the starboard beam and flying away from the boat – as most good birds are wont to do).

If you get the chance, go out on a larger vessel that is more stable, so you can use binoculars and are less likely to feel sick. Just make sure that it's going to get into deep water (>300 m, and preferably deeper). You won't see many truly pelagic seabirds (those that don't come ashore to roost) if you hug the coast. Larger vessels afford more scope for technique (on small boats you're too busy hanging on to worry about much else!). Selecting the right position is important. Find a vantage that has a wide field of vision but provides protection from the wind.

Seabirds react to ships: some avoid them while others are attracted and follow in their wake. Ship avoiders are the tough ones to see, so you need to spend most time looking in front of the vessel. Scan regularly with binoculars to locate

Seabirding equipment checklist
- **binoculars:** essential, even on small boats ✓
- **anti-nausea pills:** take one before you sail ✓
- **cold- and wet-weather gear,** even if it looks warm and sunny ✓
- **adequate protection for optics** from salty spray. Take several of your favourite lens-cleaning cloths ✓
- **protection from the sun:** sunscreen, sunglasses, and a hat that won't blow off ✓
- **plenty of food and drink** ✓

FIELD SKILLS

small birds such as storm petrels, which can be surprisingly difficult to see. Check the stern periodically to see if any interesting ship followers have appeared. Finally, look overhead now and again. Most seabirds stay low over the water, but – especially in the tropics – some species, such as frigatebirds, fly much higher.

The seabird flocks that gather to scavenge at trawlers off the western Cape are among the most spectacular in the world.

Seabirding by season

Seabirds may be seen throughout the year, but some seasons are better than others.

Many seabirds (albatrosses, petrels, skuas, Antarctic Tern) are most visible off the southern African coast in winter because they breed in the sub-Antarctic during summer. Winter is really the only time when sub-Antarctic species can be seen off Durban, and it is the time when huge numbers of sub-Antarctic species may be seen off the Cape. Foul weather, however, often causes boat trips to be cancelled.

Some species (Manx, Balearic and Cory's shearwaters, European and Leach's storm petrels, jaegers, Sabine's Gull) breed in the northern hemisphere and are visible mainly in summer. Yet other species (Great Shearwater, Black-bellied Storm Petrel, Arctic Tern) appear mainly on passage and are best sought in April–May and September–October. However, many seabirds take several years to mature so non-breeders from most species remain year round, especially further south.

The appearance of tropical species is less predictable and they occur at lower densities, but your best chance of seeing them is in late summer, especially if a cyclone pushes birds south of their normal range.

PRACTICAL BIRDING

WHERE TO BIRD

One of the joys of birding is that you can do it literally anywhere. If you are looking for birds for the first time, a suburban park or garden is as good a place as any to start because the birds are used to people and are, thus, easy to observe. Picnic sites and rest camps in national parks are good for the same reason. Wetlands are another ideal starting point because birds often gather there in numbers and they tend to be large and relatively easy to identify.

If you're looking for a specific bird, do some homework to find out the habitat(s) it prefers, where it lives within that habitat, the right time of year for migrants, and any other aids to locating the bird (e.g. time of day when it is most active, distinctive calls). You could also consult the bird atlas or locality guides (*see* 'Guides and other books', p.91) to identify areas where a particular bird has been recorded regularly in the past.

Birding in your garden

An array of birds visiting your garden is an endless source of pleasure. Your house becomes a large, fixed hide, and you may enjoy great views of birds from the comfort of your living room. No matter where you live, you can boost the attractiveness of your garden by making it a varied and safe habitat for birds.

Following these basic steps should transform your garden into a bird haven:

- **Provide diversity.** To attract a variety of birds, you need a variety of habitats. Lawns and open areas allow large birds to land and take off, and provide delights such as grubs and earthworms. Shrubs and taller trees are even more important, providing shelter, food and nest sites. If you have the space, construct a pond with shallow margins and reeds along at least one side to provide cover for shy species. Also set up a quiet area, where human disturbance is minimal. Simply making your borders broader, with plants of ascending height, creates a refuge for birds.
- **Ensure there's plenty of cover.** Small birds like to have dense cover where they can hide if they feel threatened. Providing a refuge area is ideal, but make sure that there's plenty of cover close to the house and around feeders, so birds don't feel too exposed.
- **Make water available year round.** If you don't have space for a large pond, make sure you have some water permanently in the garden. Even a small bird bath will encourage birds to visit the garden regularly. Another good idea is to include a patch of well-drained, fine soil for dust baths.
- **Don't tidy the garden obsessively.** Allow a little natural decomposition to take place. This provides a rich source of insects and other food for birds. Encourage the process by spreading lawn cuttings and other garden and kitchen waste over your beds to produce

Water features and plenty of cover make gardens attractive to birds.

a thick layer of mulch. An added bonus is that you won't have to use fertilizers. Although fertilizers have little direct impact on birds, their run-off damages wetlands.
- **Grow plants that provide food for birds.** Select plants with flowers or fruits that attract birds. Consult your local nursery, and try to plant indigenous species that are well adapted to your area and don't require much watering. If you, too, want to benefit from the bounty of your garden, you may have to cover fruit trees and vegetable gardens with netting.
- **Put out extra food.** A regular meal ticket is a sure way to attract birds. Provide a variety of foods such as seeds (different sizes), fruits (the riper the better), kitchen scraps (finely chopped), suet, bone meal and meal worms or other insects. An easy way to provide an insect meal is to leave an outside light on overnight. Deliver the food at several sites and at different levels – on the ground, on traditional bird tables, in suspended feeders and in tree trunks (wedged into the bark). Again, the greater the variety of foods, the more species you will attract. When you start out, be patient; birds take a while to learn about new food sources. And remember to feed regularly, or they might take their custom elsewhere.
- **Avoid using pesticides and other chemicals.** In addition to harming birds, pesticides rob birds of an important food source. Birds and other natural predators are a natural, cheaper and more effective way of managing garden pests. If you have to intervene, try to use natural remedies such as spraying aphids with soapy water.
- **Discourage cats and other predators.** Cats kill a surprisingly large number of garden birds. If you have a cat, put a loud bell on its collar, and encourage your cat-loving neighbours to do the same. It's not very nice to attract lots of birds to your garden merely to have them become pet food.

KEEP A GARDEN LIST
- Whether or not you make an active effort to attract birds to your garden, it's great fun to keep a garden list.
- To qualify for listing, a bird has to be seen from your garden, although some sticklers require that the birds be in or over the garden.
- Keep a list tacked onto the fridge, date each new bird, and see how long it takes you to reach milestones like 20, 50 and 100 species.

Indigenous plants tend to attract more birds – like this Scarlet-chested Sunbird.

- **Co-operate with your neighbours.** Your success will be magnified if you encourage your neighbours to join in making an area of bird-friendly habitat. Form corridors of cover along your boundaries, so that birds can move safely between gardens.
- **Provide nesting opportunities.** Many birds will breed in your garden, provided there is sufficient cover. Allow dense tangles of vegetation to develop; thick creepers are popular sites. Make sure that there's a plentiful supply of twigs and other nesting materials. You can also help by planting species that provide nest-lining such as kapok (*Eriocephalus africanus*) or even supplying feathers during the breeding season. Hole-nesting species benefit from the provision of artificial nest sites.

Nest boxes

Many birds gladly avail themselves of the opportunity to nest in artificial nest boxes. You can buy or make your own boxes, but remember to put them well off the ground and close to cover. Hollowed-out logs with entrance holes of different sizes make natural-looking nest sites. You can also leave large dead branches in the garden for birds that carve their own holes (barbets and woodpeckers). Sisal logs are excellent because their soft centre is easy for birds to hollow out. Many nurseries supply sisal logs with shallow holes already drilled into them to give birds a head start.

A nest box, strategically placed, will attract nesting birds such as owls.

Sunbird (nectar) feeders

Long used in the Americas to attract hummingbirds, nectar feeders are becoming increasingly popular for sunbirds and white-eyes. Start by placing the feeder next to a flowering shrub and try using a plastic flower around the feeder tube to help the birds learn about the new food source. You can then move it in stages until it hangs just outside a house window, allowing the birds to be viewed at distances of only a metre or so. But remember to provide some cover nearby.

You can buy feeders or make your own. They can be suspended or attached to a branch. People use sugar solutions in proportions ranging from 1:1 to 1:5 (sugar to water). It's important to change the solution regularly; otherwise, it goes off and can harm the birds. Ants and bees may be a problem. Exclude bees by making the feeder tube too narrow and deep for them to enter. Ants can be deterred by standing the feeder in a small pan of oil, or by rubbing the string from which the feeder is suspended with ant chalk (diatomaceous earth).

This is only a brief introduction to gardening for birds. For more on the subject, consult the books listed in 'Guides and other books', pp. 91–92.

Your local patch

Most birders have a favourite local birding spot – their local patch – that they visit regularly. This could be any area that combines the features of easy access and a good selection of birds. Sewage works, local dams or other wetlands are excellent locations for a local patch.

Interest in local patch birding rises where there is a regular pattern of bird movement and a chance of sighting a rarity. Unfortunately, southern Africa sits at the tip of the continent and relatively few migrant birds pass through. However, birding your local patch keeps your skills sharp, and allows you to collect useful information about the birds of your area. If you visit a particular site on a regular basis, keep good records of all birds seen (species lists with approximate numbers) as well as the time and duration of each visit, weather conditions, etc. You may not ever get around to analyzing the data, but they might prove invaluable for documenting long-term changes in bird populations.

Birding farther afield

Once you're familiar with the birds in your local area, you'll be tempted to travel to different areas in search of new birds.

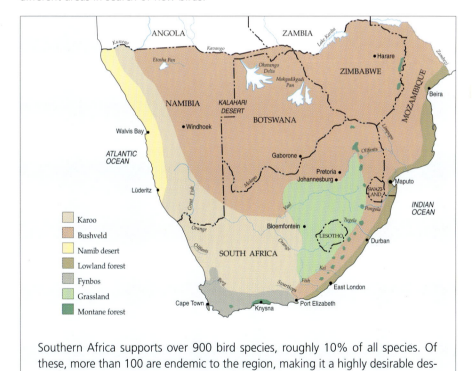

Southern Africa supports over 900 bird species, roughly 10% of all species. Of these, more than 100 are endemic to the region, making it a highly desirable destination for birders around the world. One reason for the high diversity of birds is the wide range of habitats in the region, each with its own suite of 'special' birds.

Bushveld (savanna and woodland)

Many southern African birders first become interested in birds through visits to national parks and bushveld habitats, which support a wide variety of easily spotted and identified birds. Many colourful and spectacular bird groups – vultures and other birds of prey, francolins, turacos (loeries), rollers, bee-eaters, kingfishers, hornbills, glossy starlings, sunbirds and weavers – are common.

Birding in the bushveld is good from a slow-moving vehicle as well as on foot (as long as there are no dangerous mammals about!). Birds are numerous throughout the year, but Palearctic and intra-African migrants are present only in summer. It's best to travel relatively quickly through the habitat listening for bird calls from the parties of birds that form in winter. Tits often form core members of bird parties and can be attracted by pishing or mimicking the call of a Pearl-spotted Owlet.

There are several different types of woodland within the savanna complex, ranging from arid Kalahari thornveld in the west, through more mesic mopane and teak woodlands, to miombo (Brachystegia) woodlands in Zimbabwe and Mozambique. Some birds occur throughout; others are more localized. Species richness increases to the north and east.

Lilac-breasted Roller

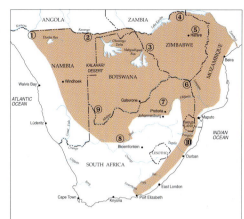

ENDEMIC SPECIES

Because the habitat extends north of the Zambezi, there are relatively few bushveld species that are endemic to southern Africa. The following are found mostly in arid western bushveld: **Red-billed Francolin, Burchell's Sandgrouse, Bradfield's Hornbill, Monotonous Lark, Kalahari Robin, Barred Warbler, Marico Flycatcher, Crimson-breasted** and **Southern White-crowned shrikes, Cape** and **Burchell's Glossy Starlings, Shaft-tailed Whydah, Violet-eared Waxbill.**

> **Top 10 birding sites – bushveld**
> 1 Ruacana, 2 Rundu-Mahango, 3 Hwange, 4 Zambezi Valley, 5 Marondera, 6 Punda Maria, 7 Nylsvlei, 8 Rooipoort, 9 Kalagadi Park, 10 Mkuze Game Reserve.

The **White-throated Robin-chat** occurs farther east, and the **Short-clawed Lark** is localized in arid thornveld in South Africa and eastern Botswana; the **Boulder Chat** in Zimbabwe, western Mozambique and eastern Botswana; and the **Lemon-breasted Canary** occupies dry savannas in eastern South Africa, Zimbabwe and Mozambique.

Finally, there are several endemics restricted to the arid savannas of northern Namibia and southern Angola: **Hartlaub's Francolin, Rüppell's Parrot, Monteiro's Hornbill, Violet Woodhoopoe, Carp's Black Tit, Bare-cheeked Babbler, Rockrunner**.

Within southern Africa, many species are only found in Zimbabwe and Mozambique: **Racket-tailed Roller, Green-backed Honeybird, Whyte's Barbet, Miombo** and **Rufous-bellied tits, Miombo Rock Thrush, Chestnut-fronted Helmet Shrike, Lesser Blue-eared Starling, Miombo Double-collared, Yellow-bellied, Coppery** and **Western Violet-backed sunbirds, Black-eared Canary, Cabanis's Bunting.**

Southern Ground Hornbill

Forest

There are two types of forest: afromontane and coastal. Forests are the smallest terrestrial biome in the region, but they support a large number of sought-after and spectacular birds such as Crowned Eagle, Narina Trogon, Emerald Cuckoo and Green Twinspot.

Virtually all forest birding is on foot. Stick to forest trails as much as possible to limit the noise you make while walking. Try to look over the canopy to get a better view of canopy specials such as Bronze-naped Pigeon. Again, species richness is greatest in the north-east. Afromontane forest generally supports fewer species than coastal forest, although many species occur in both.

Forest birding is challenging, and forest birds are often hard to locate. Knowledge of calls is perhaps most important here, and judicious use of tapes can help in locating elusive species. (In light of the small Green Barbet population at Ngoye, birders should avoid using tapes to call up this bird as much as possible).

Season is not too important, although birds tend to be more vocal in spring-summer (main breeding season), and some birds leave higher-elevation forests in winter. The time of day is more significant, with a marked peak in singing in the early morning. Given the dense vegetation, many species are best located by their calls.

ENDEMIC SPECIES
The following are endemic to southern Africa: **Cape Parrot**, **Knysna Turaco** (Loerie), **Bush Blackcap**,

Top 10 birding sites – forest
1 Chinaziua, 2 Haroni-Rusitu, 3 Vumba, 4 Woodbush, 5 Cape Vidal, 6 Ndumu, 7 Ngoye, 8 Weza, 9 Dwesa, 10 Nature's Valley.

PRACTICAL BIRDING

Chorister and **Brown robin-chats**, **Knysna Warbler**, **Olive Bush Shrike** and **Forest Canary**.

Rudd's Apalis, **Neergaard's Sunbird** and **Pink-throated Twinspot** are restricted to sand forest and thickets in Zululand and southern Mozambique. **Chirinda Apalis** and **Roberts' Warbler** are found only in the afromontane forests in the eastern highlands of Zimbabwe. The **Green Barbet** (sometimes treated as an endemic species, **Woodward's Barbet**) is highly localized within southern Africa, being restricted to Ngoye forest in KwaZulu-Natal.

Chorister Robin-chat

Grasslands

After wetlands, grasslands are the most threatened habitat in southern Africa. Large areas have been transformed for agriculture and forestry, and as a result the birds that inhabit these areas are among the region's most threatened species. Grasslands occur at high elevation in the eastern half of South Africa and Lesotho, with a small area in Zimbabwe from Harare to the eastern highlands. These areas also support some of the best wetlands in the region.

Searching for the larger grassland birds is best done from a car, but to see several of the smaller species (e.g. Melodious, Rudd's and Botha's larks and Yellow-breasted Pipit) you need to be on foot. Be sure to ask for permission before venturing onto private land. Spring-summer is the best time to visit because the larks are singing. In winter, many species are in non-breeding plumage, and the birds' movements are less predictable.

Grasslands support a number of endemics and several other, quite spectacular birds, including all three cranes (Blue, Southern Crowned, Wattled), Stanley's Bustard, Blue Swallow and Long-tailed Widowbird.

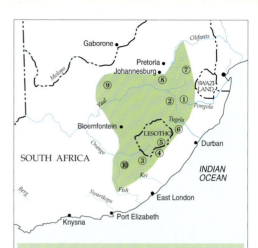

Southern Bald Ibis

Top 10 birding sites – grassland
Most birders work the area around 1 Wakkerstroom, where the birds are fairly well staked out. (The 'Wild Turkey' in Wakkerstroom sells a bird guide and provides general information for visitors.) Other good areas include 2 Memel, 3 Naude's Neck, 4 Matatiele Mountain, 5 Sani Pass, 6 Giant's Castle, 7 Dullstroom to Belfast, 8 Suikerbosrand, 9 Bloemhof to Sweizer-Reineke, and 10 Molteno. Many other areas in the Eastern Cape, Free State and North-West Province also offer good grassland birding from secondary roads.

Lammergeier or Bearded Vulture

ENDEMIC SPECIES

The eastern Free State, the escarpment of Mpumulanga and adjacent KwaZulu-Natal form the most diverse grassland habitat for birds and are home to a host of endemics including: **Southern Bald Ibis, Blue Korhaan, Rudd's** and **Botha's larks** (very localized), **Eastern Long-billed Lark, Buff-streaked Chat, Drakensberg Prinia, Yellow-breasted Pipit, Gurney's Sugarbird.**

The montane grasslands of Lesotho have a remnant population of **Lammergeiers** as well as several other southern African endemics: **Orange-breasted Rockjumper, Mountain Pipit, Drakensberg Siskin.** Other endemics that have the core of their ranges in the grasslands include: **Jackal Buzzard, Red-winged** and **Grey-winged francolins, Southern White-bellied Korhaan, Melodious Lark, Sentinel Rock Thrush, Cape Longclaw, Pied Starling.**

Fynbos

The Cape Floral Kingdom, the smallest of the world's six floral kingdoms, extends from the mountains around Vanrhynsdorp south to Cape Town and east to Port Elizabeth. Large tracts of mountain fynbos (literally 'fine-leaved bush') remain on the coastal fold mountains, albeit threatened by invasive alien plants such as pines and wattles. The coastal lowlands, which support a mix of vegetation types such as lowland fynbos, renosterveld and coastal thicket, have been largely transformed into agricultural and residential areas. The fynbos is at its best in early spring, although the weather at this time is changeable. The mountain areas support good numbers of Peregrine Falcon and Booted and Verreaux's eagles, as well as the elusive Striped Flufftail. For most species, birding is best on foot. You may need a tape to locate Victorin's Warbler.

Cape Sugarbird

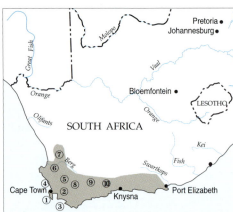

Top 10 birding sites – fynbos
1 Cape Point, 2 Sir Lowry's Pass, 3 Harold Porter Gardens (Betty's Bay), 4 Paarl Mountain, 5 Bainskloof, 6 Piketberg Mountain, 7 Cedarberg, 8 Dassieshoek Nature Reserve (Robertson), 9 Boosmansbos, 10 Swartberg Pass. For good lowland fynbos birding visit the West Coast National Park, Columbine Peninsula, Lambert's Bay, Tienie Versveld Wild Flower Reserve (Darling) and De Hoop Nature Reserve.

ENDEMIC SPECIES

Despite its immense floral diversity, mountain fynbos, with its low-nutrient soils, supports few birds. Only seven species are endemic: **Cape Sugarbird, Orange-breasted Sunbird, Cape Siskin, Hottentot Buttonquail, Cape Rockjumper, Victorin's Warbler, Protea Canary.** Only the first four of these species occur on the Cape Peninsula.

Six endemic species are restricted to the coastal lowlands: **Cape Francolin, Southern Black Korhaan, Agulhas Clapper Lark, Cape** and **Agulhas long-billed larks, Cape Bulbul.** All are common and can be found fairly easily by driving the quieter, secondary roads. Other birds to look out for are the **Black Harrier, Blue Crane** and **Stanley's Bustard.**

Several other endemic species have the core of their ranges in this biome: **Knysna Woodpecker** and **Southern Tchagra** occur in coastal thicket from the Cape to southern Natal, whereas **Ground Woodpecker, Cape Rock-thrush, Cape Grassbird** and **Cape Weaver** extend into the karoo and grassland biomes.

Karoo

Although the north-east of southern Africa has more bird species, the 'special' birds (those that are found only in southern Africa) are concentrated in the arid west. They reach their greatest diversity in the Karoo. Contrary to popular opinion, there's plenty to recommend birding this area, not least the stunning array of larks.

The Karoo forms the major part of western South Africa and southern Namibia, with grassy nama karoo in the east and shrub-dominated succulent karoo in the west. Because the land is used predominantly for extensive grazing, the landscape is less transformed than in many other biomes, making much of the area suitable for birding.

Like other open-country biomes, the Karoo is best birded from a car, with regular stops and short walks. Species such as Cinnamon-breasted Warbler and Sclater's Lark are patchily distributed and it may take some effort to locate them. Spring is probably the best time to visit; it gets too hot in summer and can be bitterly cold in winter. It's good to get an early start because the birds keep a low

Top 10 birding sites – Karoo
1 Karoopoort, 2 Katbakkies, 3 Karoo National Park, 4 Brandvlei, 5 Kenhardt to Pofadder, 6 Aggenys dunes, 7 Aardvark Kloof, 8 Port Nolloth, 9 Richtersveld National Park, 10 the area around Aus.

Namaqua Sandgrouse

profile in the heat of the day, and the heat haze precludes scanning for distant birds. Travelling aside, the best use of time in the heat of the day is to check watering points for birds coming in to drink.

A wide variety of birds of prey, ranging from the massive Martial Eagle to the diminutive Pygmy Falcon, may be seen in this habitat.

ENDEMIC SPECIES

Among the many birds virtually restricted to the Karoo are: **Karoo Korhaan, Rosy-faced Lovebird, White-backed Mousebird, Karoo Chat, Sickle-winged Chat, Karoo Robin, Karoo Eremomela, Fairy Flycatcher, Cinnamon-breasted, Namaqua** and **Rufous-eared warblers, African Rock Pipit, Pale-winged Starling, Dusky Sunbird, White-throated Seed-eater, Black-headed Canary, Lark-like Bunting**. But it's the larks that are most spectacular: **Large-billed, Karoo, Red, Barlow's, Karoo Long-billed, Sclater's** and **Stark's larks** and **Grey-backed** and **Black-eared sparrow larks** are all endemic, with another 10 or so with ranges that extend beyond the boundary of the Karoo.

The range of many other southern African endemics centres on the Karoo: **Pale Chanting Goshawk, Black Harrier, Ludwig's Bustard, Northern Black Korhaan, Burchell's Courser, Namaqua Sandgrouse, Red-eyed Bulbul, Southern Grey Tit, Cape Penduline Tit, Ant-eating** and **Mountain chats, Layard's** and **Chestnut-vented titbabblers, Spotted** and **Black-chested prinias, Fiscal Flycatcher, Cape** and **Great sparrows, Sociable Weaver, Red-headed** and **Scaly-feathered finches.**

Desert

True desert is restricted to the Namib coast of Namibia. The Namib Desert is justly famous for its stunning landscapes and towering dune seas. Most birds of the open plains are best located by driving slowly along, and stopping to scan and listen. Dune Larks require a walk into the vegetated dunes, and most of the escarpment species are best located on foot. Apart from endemics, there are spectacular birds to be seen, including Lappet-faced Vulture and Red-necked Falcon.

Double-banded Courser

Time of day is more important than season. Get out birding at the crack of dawn; retire for a siesta or alternatively work the coastal wetlands when the day gets hot.

ENDEMIC SPECIES

Relatively few birds occur in the true desert, but there are several endemics such as **Rüppell's Korhaan**, and **Dune** and **Gray's larks** as well as the very pale Namib form of **Tractrac Chat**. The escarpment that forms the inner boundary of the desert supports several other endemics, notably: **Bradfield's Swift**, **Benguela Long-billed Lark** (north of Brandberg), **Herero Chat**, **White-tailed Shrike**.

Top 10 birding sites – desert
1 The Koichab River inland of Lüderitz, 2 Sossusvlei, 3 the gravel plains of the Namib-Naukluft Park, 4 the Naukluft Mountains, 5 Rooibank south of Walvis Bay, 6 Spitskop, 7 the Erongo Mountains west of Omaruru, 8 Brandberg, 9 Khorixas, 10 Kaokoland.

Herero Chat

Wetlands

Southern African wetlands come in all shapes and sizes, from seasonal wetlands (vleis or dambos) to the Kariba Dam, and from tiny streams to the mighty Zambezi River. Freshwater wetlands are concentrated in the eastern half of southern Africa owing to the higher rainfall. Because large numbers of birds of many species aggregate at wetlands, they are popular birding sites, and certainly among the best areas for introducing people to birding. There are few other habitats where you can see as many species at the same time and as many large and attractive birds. Permanent hides allow a number of birders to enjoy together great views of a variety of birds.

Wetlands are under ever-increasing pressure from humans both for recreation and as a source of water. Fortunately, thanks to southern Africa's

Top 10 birding sites – wetlands
1 Okavango delta, 2 Chobe-upper Zambezi complex, 3 Rainham Dam and the Harare vleis, 4 Zambezi delta, 5 Nylsvlei,
6 Marievale, 7 Nsumu pan and the Mkuze River floodplain, 8 Franklin marsh,
9 Wilderness lakes, 10 Strandfontein sewage works.

Lesser Jacana

South African Shelduck

unpredictable rainfall, waterbirds are used to moving around with the appearance and disappearance of wetlands. As a result, they are not as severely impacted by humans as are many freshwater animals and plants.

Although season is immaterial, wetlands are better visited in summer, when there is a large influx of Palearctic waders and terns. The most challenging to grip are the skulking rails, crakes, flufftails and bitterns. Some crakes and some other wetland birds, such as the Black Coucal, are intra-African migrants and arrive only in years of above-average rainfall. Seeing these species often requires several trips to the vleis around Harare.

ENDEMIC SPECIES
A consequence of the high mobility of wetland species is that only three are endemic (or nearly endemic) to southern Africa: **Slaty Egret, South African Shelduck, Cape Shoveller.**

The coastline, islands and estuaries

Offshore islands occur between central Namibia and Algoa Bay. They are extremely important as predator-free breeding localities for sea birds and other coastal birds. The estuaries and sheltered bays along the southern African coast attract many birds, including large populations of migrant Palearctic waders and terns. Estuaries and coastal wetlands are hot spots for vagrant shore birds, gulls and terns. Virtually any estuary with extensive mud flats is worth checking.

Most of the coastline is exposed and supports smaller numbers of coastal birds. The oceanic waters off southern Africa attract a diverse array of pelagic seabirds from around the world.

There's no specific season for birding along the coast, although migrant numbers peak in summer and Damara Terns are absent in winter. Foraging by coastal and estuarine birds is regulated by tidal cycles rather than time of day, so plan your birding according to the tides. At most sites, birding is best at the mid-point of high tide, when birds gather close to shore or move to high-tide roosts.

Top 10 birding sites – coastal

To date, the best sites for vagrants have been 1 Cunene River Mouth, 2 the Hoanib and other river mouths along the Skeleton Coast, 3 Walvis Bay lagoon, 4 Berg River, 5 Langebaan lagoon, 6 Gamtoos River, 7 Swartkops River, 8 Durban Bay and Blue Lagoon, 9 Mvoti River mouth and 10 Richard's Bay. The offshore islands provide impressive displays of sea birds. Bird Island, Lambert's Bay is the easiest site to reach, although Malgas Island is arguably more impressive. Robben Island and Boulders Beach have large African Penguin colonies.

Damara Tern

ENDEMIC SPECIES

Several coastal birds are endemic to the cold upwelling waters of the Benguela Current and adjacent south coast: **African Penguin, Bank, Cape** and **Crowned Cormorants, African Black Oystercatcher, Hartlaub's Gull**. The subspecies of **Kelp Gull**, endemic to southern Africa, differs structurally from other subspecies, and may be another (endemic) species: **Cape Gull**. **Cape Gannets** and **Damara Terns** are breeding endemics that disperse north along the west coast of Africa during the non-breeding season.

African Black Oystercatcher

The world's your oyster

Once you've explored southern Africa, you can broaden your horizons and venture north into Africa or travel to see some exotic birds on other continents. Little can compare with the thrill of landing on a new continent where virtually every bird is new. It's like starting birding all over again.

Deciding where to go depends on your budget and your personal taste in birds. But here are some points to consider, and some tips on planning a trip:

The Swallow-tailed Gull is restricted to the west coast of South America.

- **Field guides.** It's much easier to go birding in a country that has a reasonable field guide. It's very frustrating not being able to identify the birds you see.
- **Good locality information.** Pioneering a poorly documented area is rewarding, but it requires a lot of preparation. Most developed countries have their own guides. Nigel Wheatley's where-to-watch guides cover Africa, Asia and South America (*see* 'Guides and other books, pp. 91–92). Athough not very detailed, they give you an idea of the birds and sites in each country.
- **Other sources of information.** Chat to other birders who have visited the area and get hold of trip reports. This gives a realistic feel of what is and isn't possible.
- **When to go.** When choosing your destination, factor in the weather (which may or may not be conducive to birding), the presence of migrants (which can add considerably to your list of birds), whether birds will be calling (ground-rollers in Madagascar, for instance, are very tricky to see when not calling), and whether birds will be in breeding plumage (a great deal of identification heartache may result from arriving out of the breeding season).
- **Advance planning.** Have a good idea of your route, and make bookings for sites where bookings are required. If you're planning to rent a car, try to do so before you get there.
- **Visa and health requirements.** Make sure you have all the right documentation before leaving home. Health insurance is a worthwhile precaution.

> ### Trip reports
> Trip reports are an invaluable source of information. They are single-visit, informal where-to-watch guides. Although they may not cover all sites, they give a realistic idea of what you can expect to see. Good trip reports have sketch maps of birding locations, species lists for each site, as well as useful tips on travel and accommodation. The African Bird Club offers trip reports for Africa. Surf the Internet or contact the Foreign Bird Reports and Information Service. (*See* 'Addresses and other useful information', pp. 90–93.)

BIRDING 6 SOCIALLY

For many people, birding is a social activity. The successful combination of birding and socializing depends, partly, on the nature of the habitat. The main drawback to birding socially is that groups of people tend to make more noise (especially if there's some socializing going on!) and, thus, are likely to disturb the birds. This objection falls away in car-based birding, where the source of disturbance is the vehicle, irrespective of the number of people in it. Indeed, in a car, the more eyes the better (as long as you don't get shoe-horned into the middle of the back seat).

Seabirding and, to a lesser extent, wader spotting, can also be more enjoyable with a few companions to keep the enthusiasm going. But when it comes to forest birding, fewer is generally better, especially if there is only a narrow trail. Having the person in front see twice as many birds as those following is a sure way to disrupt group harmony.

The other factor to consider when mixing socializing and birding is the seriousness of the situation. If you're pottering round your local patch for the umpteenth time, you might quite enjoy chatting to a couple of mates. But if you're on the trail of an elusive lifer, the last thing you want is other birders getting in the way.

Whether birding alone or in a group, almost all birders gain considerable pleasure from chatting to other birders about their experiences. Indeed, although they would probably deny this, many gain the greatest pleasure from 'gripping off' their mates! By joining a bird club, you instantly become part of a group of like-minded people who find nothing more fascinating than debating the finer points of pipit identification, or arguing about the latest rumour about a possible split.

Bird clubs

Bird clubs are especially useful for beginners because they arrange outings, evening talks and other activities that help to improve birding skills. They provide useful information through club newsletters, magazines and journals – an outlet, moreover, for publication of your more exciting observations.

There are more than 60 local bird clubs in South Africa. They play an important role in lobbying at the local level for conservation issues and, through the umbrella body BirdLife South Africa, on a national scale. (For addresses, see pp. 90–91.) Members of branch clubs of BirdLife South Africa may choose to receive the popular birding magazine *Africa: Birds & Birding* and the scientific journal *Ostrich*, as well as national and local club newsletters.

Leading birding groups

If you are leading a group of birders, brief the group beforehand on your general plans, the types of birds you're likely to encounter, as well as the type of terrain and length of any walks. Try to select an area or habitat that's conducive to group birding. Open habitats and wetlands are ideal. If you must venture into a forest or other dense habitats, select wide paths so that everyone has a good chance to see each bird. Get everyone to stand still and be quiet if you're attempting to lure a bird into view. A laser pointer is effective for indicating the position of birds skulking on the forest floor.

Use telescopes to show people birds that they are struggling to locate. If you visit a reserve that has hides, approach the hide as quietly as possible. Sit back from the hide's viewing slot and instruct everyone to move slowly and quietly within the hide. Under no circumstances should anyone point out of a hide to indicate a bird, because the birds are likely to depart in a hurry.

Listing and big days

Whether they tick off birds in their field guides, use the latest birding software package, or merely file away information in the recesses of their brains, birders generally keep lists of the birds they have seen. Unfortunately, listing has gained a bad reputation because some birders are very competitive about the size of their bird lists, be they global, regional, lifetime or annual. One problem is that the size of your list is often more indicative of your wealth than your birding ability.

A small section of a big twitch in the UK

The American Birding Association (*www.americanbirding.org*) encourages listing by publishing annually the numbers of birds people have seen in each state, country and region. Some birders in southern Africa attach great significance to being a member of the '800 club' of people who have seen more than 800 species within the region (visit *www.zestforbirds.co.za*).

One form of competitive birding that is great fun, and raises significant amounts of money for bird conservation, is a sponsored Big Bird Day. The rules are simple: teams of three to four birders compete to see who can see or hear the most species within a 24-hour period. A majority of team members (i.e. two out of three or three out of four) has to see or hear each species for the team to count it in its total. Money is raised by asking people to commit themselves to a specific amount per bird recorded.

Big days are great fun, generating lots of excitement and adrenaline. They're also pretty exhausting, so that once a year is more than enough for most people. Very often, the list of birds not seen is more interesting than the list of those you do see. Big days can be tackled by birders at any level of experience, and range from pleasantly relaxed affairs to frantic scrambles for the full 24 hours. Some teams set additional hurdles, such as remaining at one site, or within one-quarter degree square, or only counting birds identified by sound. To obtain a large total requires careful planning, lots of energy and a certain amount of luck.

Planning a big birding day

Successful big day teams plan the event with military precision. The first decision to make is what route to follow. You want to cover as many habitats as possible, but to minimize the amount of time spent travelling. You also have to consider at what time of day you'll visit each site. Although it would be ideal to visit all sites in the early morning, you have to prioritize habitats where birds are hardest to find at other times of the day. This generally means being in forests at dawn, and tackling open habitats and wetlands later in the day. If your route is in an urban area, consider the likely traffic problems; if you're on the coast, take into account the state of the tide.

Once the route has been decided, it's essential to spend a few days going over the route, checking the time it takes to travel between sites and staking out tricky species. Finding nests is one way to ensure that a bird will be available. Make sure you're well rested before the big day itself, have enough food and drink to keep going on the day, and see that you have all the equipment ready (especially tapes). It's often a good idea not to start at midnight and, instead, to leave most of the night birding for the evening, when you're likely to see more birds.

To tick or not to tick ...

You can count a bird for your life list only if you see it alive in the wild; dead birds, zoos and television don't count. Beyond this simple rule lies a grey area where personal ethics come into play. Although some listers are happy to take another's word, most birders prefer to identify for themselves every bird that they tick. Pressure on you to bend your principles increases, however, with the rarity of the bird and the number of people who grip you off. For example, you're in a group of birders that flushes a bird. All you see is a blurred silhouette – but those closer to the action identify it as a rare flufftail. Strictly speaking, you shouldn't tick it, but the chances of seeing it again are slim, and everyone else is celebrating and ...

Another moral dilemma is the question of birds in mist nets. You should not tick birds caught in nets. But how soon after release do they become acceptable? Many birders won't tick a bird until at least 24 hours after release; others are less fussy. These debates can become ridiculous. One tale (possibly apocryphal) is of two car-loads of birders driving at night somewhere in the depths of South America. The first car hits a nightjar. Stopping to investigate, the dead bird turns out to be a very rare species. Argument ensues as to whether occupants of the second car can tick the bird, because it's uncertain whether the bird was dead when it bounced off the lead car into the lights of the second car!

If you're uncertain about whether a bird is 'tickable', you can always submit your case to the American Birding Association's Recording Standards and Ethics Committee, who have a long list of complex rules and regulations.

Birding chat groups

The computer-literate birder now has access to a large audience through birding chat groups on the Internet. South Africa has three chat groups:
- SA Bird Net: sabirdnet@und.ac.za (to subscribe send a message: subscribe sabirdnet [your name] to majordomo@und.ac.za)
- two regional chat groups (Cape Bird Net and Pretoria Bird Net)

Other regional chat groups that often have interesting discussion topics include:
- Europe: ukbirdnet@dcs.bbk.ac.uk; ebn@otax.tky.hut.fi
- North America: birdchat@listserv.arizona.edu (to subscribe send a message: subscribe BIRDCHAT [your name] to listserv@listserv.arizona.edu)
- Australia: birding-aus@deakin.edu.au

In some of these groups, only members are allowed to post messages. If you do join a chat group, be prepared to receive large numbers of messages every day.

PRACTICAL BIRDING

ADVANCED BIRDING

If birding grips you, you'll no longer be satisfied with identifying large, colourful and conspicuous birds. The challenge of adding cryptic LBJs (little brown jobs) to your life list and the tantalizing possibility of finding a rarity will lure you into more complicated areas of bird identification.

To meet this challenge you will have to hone your identification skills and add to your stock of birding equipment.

Advanced identification

When identifying birds, bear in mind that there are three types of identification features:
- Absolute characters are checked easily and identification is usually straightforward (e.g. species A has a white rump, species B does not).
- Relative characters rely on comparative knowledge of both of the species involved (e.g. species A has a heavier bill than species B).
- Variable characters are indicative but not absolutely diagnostic (e.g. species A typically – but not always – has streaked flanks, whereas species B typically – but not always – lacks flank streaks).

For identification purposes, absolute characters are more useful (or convincing) than relative characters, which, in turn, are more useful than variable characters. When attempting to identify a bird, or to convince other birders that your identification is correct, first check for absolute characters and then for relative and variable characters.

Most birds can be identified to species quite easily by one or more absolute characters. It is unusual for all individuals within a species to lack any absolute characters (but *see* Splits and Lumps, p. 72) because the birds themselves need visible or audible cues to recognize potential mates and competitors.

Tricky problems

However, absolute characters are often present only in certain sexes and at certain ages (male weavers, for instance, are relatively easy to identify in breeding plumage, but can be a nightmare to identify during the rest of the year).

In other species, the diagnostic character may not always be observable (a silent individual, for instance, of a species where the call is diagnostic). Another problem is species that are highly variable, including many raptors and some albatrosses. You have to accept that individual birds cannot always be identified with certainty.

To identify tricky species requires experience, patience and practice. Careful study of fine plumage detail can resolve many identification conundrums. For instance, to identify some waders you need to first age the bird, based on feather details, before you can identify it to species. Top birders now use characters that until recently were used only to

Seen in active moult this Mountain Chat looks mottled and dishevelled.

Old, worn wing feathers give this immature Kelp Gull a paler brown wing patch.

identify birds in the hand (e.g. relative lengths of primary feathers). Clearly, this requires a very good view, preferably through a telescope.

Jizz is extremely important in identifying birds whose absolute characters are not apparent. Spend time getting to know all the variations (age and sex) in the common species in your area. The more you know about the commonly encountered species, the more likely you are to spot something unusual.

While no two species are exactly alike in terms of proportions, posture, flight action, etc., individuals also differ within species and a bird can change its shape and posture dramatically depending on its circumstances. When it's cold, birds often fluff out their plumage to maximize insulation, making them look fat and dumpy, whereas they look tall and sleek when it's hot. Moult, also, can change the shape of a bird quite dramatically.

European Roller: under normal conditions looking sleek and tall (left) and fluffed out against the cold, looking rounder and unkempt (right).

You also have to consider abnormal individuals. Some individuals have growth abnormalities, such as bills that continue to grow, or are crossed. Another, often spectacular but rare, example is the suite of pigmentation abnormalities ranging from albinism to melanism (*see* 'Coloration abnormalities', p. 71). These are normally the result of rare mutations, but can also result from changes in diet making new pigments available.

In one celebrated example, young Cedar Waxwings in the United States started to develop orange, not yellow, tail tips because of the abundance of an introduced plant that fruited while their tails were moulting. (Carotenoids, responsible for most red- and yellow-coloured feathers, derive from a bird's diet.) Only the young birds were affected because they moult at a different time from the adults.

Many raptors have two colour morphs, as seen in this pair of Tawny Eagles.

Pollen can give birds like this Cape White-eye a yellow face.

A WORD OF ADVICE
Be critical of your own observations. Does the bird look large simply because it's closer than you think, or because it's next to a particularly small bird? Is the colour you see affected by prevailing light conditions? Colours look very different in mellow evening light than they do in the middle of the day. Are you missing features because the bird is back-lit or in moult? Is the bird's posture or flight action peculiar owing to strong wind?

Other abnormalities may result from hybridization. Although cross-breeding is rare, more than 10 per cent of the world's birds have been reported to hybridize occasionally. Their hybrid offspring tend to be intermediate in size and colour, and can pose real identification problems. A more prosaic problem arises from staining of the plumage or bare parts. Birds feeding on nectar often develop a yellow crown or face from pollen, and in many shore birds, mud may mask the colour of the legs and bill. Abnormal feather wear can also make individuals look unusual.

If faced with a tricky identification problem, don't rely solely on field guides. Good field guides illustrate the main plumages and highlight the main identification criteria, but they cannot hope to be comprehensive, especially for species that have complex plumage development stretching over a number of years. And don't always believe the field guides; sometimes they are simply wrong! If you take identification seriously, you will, on occasion, have to check handbooks such as *Birds of Africa* (*see* p. 92) and other, more detailed, sources of information, or perhaps visit your local museum to check specific features on skins. Much information on tricky identification problems is published in birding magazines.

Finding rarities

Finding rare birds can be one of the most exciting experiences in birding. It's right up there with cracking 50 or so lifers a day in a new area. Serious ornithologists often dismiss rarities as biologically insignificant, and thus of little interest, but that doesn't detract from the thrill of finding something totally unexpected. Indeed, for many birders, it's the challenge of finding something new that keeps their interest in local birding alive.

Birds are highly mobile creatures and – with all that moving about – there's always a chance that individual birds will get lost and end up in the most unlikely places. One has only to look at the amazing list of vagrants that have been recorded in Britain over the last few decades to realize that virtually any bird can pitch up at your local patch. Some species, however, are more likely to turn up than others. Typically, species that migrate or are nomadic are more likely to wander than are resident species.

There's no sure-fire recipe for finding rarities, but there are some ways to boost your chances of success. First and foremost, you have to spend time in the field. You won't find anything exciting if you don't look. Some habitats, however, are more productive than others because they support migrant or nomadic birds. Being at the tail end of migration

WHAT IF?

... you encounter a bird that's not in the field guide at all? More often than not, it'll be an exotic bird that has escaped from captivity, but there's always a chance of finding a species new to the region. It's best to report the unusual bird to a more experienced birder as soon as possible, so that the sighting can be confirmed. You can mail a message (ideally with a description of the bird) to the SA Rare Bird Alert (sararebirdalert@egroups.com). See 'Guides and other books', p. 91 for books that will help you identify the bird yourself.

Coloration abnormalities

albinism: the total absence of pigmentation throughout; pink eyes and legs. Very rare in wild birds because affected individuals generally die. Most so-called 'albinos' are actually leucistic.

leucism: the absence of pigments from all or part of the plumage, but with at least some pigmentation on soft parts such as the iris, bill or legs.

melanism: an overabundance of the feather pigment melanin, resulting in darker than normal plumage. Related abnormalities are **erythrism**, an excess of reddish pigments, and **xanthochroism**, an excess of yellow pigments.

schizochroism: the absence of one type of pigment, or a chemical change in pigment structure resulting in the appearance of a different colour (e.g. yellow forms of Crimson-breasted Boubou and Black-collared Barbet).

bilateral gynandromorphs: This is an exceptionally rare abnormality where half the body assumes male plumage, the other female. It's usually detectable only in sexually dimorphic species.

The rare yellow-headed form of the Black-collared Barbet (right) is an example of schizochroism.

Splits and Lumps

Bird populations vary across their ranges, and it is not always easy to decide where one species stops and another starts. As the debate swings back and forth, populations are alternately lumped together into one species, then split into several species.

The Biological Species Concept (BSC), almost universally adopted from the 1930s to the 1980s, defines a species as a distinct group of individuals that are able to interbreed. The problem with this definition is that, increasingly, individuals from one species are found to have interbred with individuals from other species and to have produced viable offspring. Also, it is not possible to test the status of isolated populations, such as Grey-headed Gulls in Africa and in South America. They look the same, but we cannot test whether they interbreed, because they never meet.

Over the last decade or so, the Phylogenetic Species Concept (PSC) has been gaining support. It defines species as groups of individuals that share at least one common, derived character (i.e. a character that has evolved recently). This raises new problems. For example, Grey-headed Gulls in Africa and Grey-headed Gulls in South America would be regarded as two species, but were a vagrant South American Grey-headed Gull to arrive on the west coast of Africa, a birder would have no way of telling it from the local African Grey-headed Gull.

Application of the PSC has led to many more splits than lumps. Increasing use of the PSC means that birders will have to accept that not all birds can be identified to species level.

Old species	New species
Wandering Albatross	Wandering/Tristan Albatross
Yellow-nosed Albatross	Atlantic/Indian Yellow-nosed Albatross
White-chinned Petrel	White-chinned/Spectacled Petrel
Black Kite	Yellow-billed/Black Kite
Black-rumped Button-quail	Black-rumped/Hottentot Button-quail
Black Korhaan	Southern/Northern Black Korhaan
Lesser Golden Plover	American/ Pacific Golden Plover
Knysna Turaco (Loerie)	Knysna/Livingstone's/Schalow's Turaco
Lesser Cuckoo	Lesser/Madagascar Cuckoo
Burchell's Coucal	Burchell's/White-browed Coucal
Clapper Lark	Cape/Agulhas/Eastern Clapper Lark
Karoo/Dune Lark	Karoo/Barlow's/Dune Lark
Long-billed Lark	Cape/Agulhas/Karoo/Eastern/Benguela Long-billed Lark
Rufous-bellied Tit	Rufous-bellied/Cinnamon-bellied Tit
Bleating Warbler	Green-backed/Grey-backed Camaroptera
Black-backed Cisticola	Black-backed/Rufous-winged Cisticola
Spotted Prinia	Spotted/Drakensberg Prinia
Olive Sunbird	Eastern/Western Olive Sunbird
Grey-headed Sparrow	Southern/Northern Grey-headed Sparrow

routes (at least for land birds), southern Africa lacks vagrant traps such as the various points, peninsulas and offshore islands in Europe and North America that are famous for vagrants.

Locally, wetlands and marine environments are the best bet for finding rarities, the highest levels of vagrancy being those for shore birds and seabirds. The best sites in southern Africa are probably the isolated wetlands on the desert coast of Namibia, where vagrant birds in the area tend to aggregate. Spring and summer are the best times for looking for birds from the northern hemisphere (waders and gulls), and autumn and winter are best for birds, such as the American Purple Gallinule and sub-Antarctic seabirds, from other regions in the southern hemisphere. However, vagrants can turn up anywhere, and the vigilant birder may be rewarded at any time.

A NOTE OF CAUTION

Don't get so caught up in the excitement of finding rare birds that your imagination starts to twist the facts. One of a birder's most prized assets is his/her reputation. If you start to see a lot of rare birds that are never seen by other birders, you run the risk of being called a 'stringer'. And once you get that reputation, you might as well take up another hobby because it's going to be almost impossible to get anyone to take you or your records seriously.

Reporting rarities

After getting the word out quickly via the SA Rare Bird Alert (sararebirdalert@egroups.com), submit a description of any rarity for ratification by the South African Rarities Committee. Accepted records are published in *Africa: Birds & Birding*. A standard form is available from most bird clubs. It asks for information about the species, location, date, light conditions, optical aids, other species present, your previous experience of the species, etc. The most important sections require a detailed description of the bird and specific reasons why similar species were eliminated.

When describing a rarity, the most common mistake is to describe the circumstances of the sighting without providing a detailed description. You must describe every feature of the bird that you saw. In the section on similar species, list the species that could be confused with the bird in question and emphasize the diagnostic characters that distinguish your bird from each similar species. Substantiate your record by attaching a copy of the field notes you made at the time, before referring to any guides. Having a photograph of the bird, however fuzzy and distant, helps enormously.

Rüppell's Griffon – a regional rarity

Advanced equipment

Once you're deep into the joys of birding, you'll want to consider investing in a telescope, tripod, recording equipment and, perhaps, a camera.

Telescopes

After binoculars, a telescope is perhaps the most important piece of birding equipment. There is little to compare with the pleasure of getting really up close and personal with a bird through a quality scope.

The diversity of scopes isn't quite as daunting as that of binoculars, but there's still a wide selection to choose from. In general, avoid anything advertised as an astronomical telescope. Most birders use refractive telescopes or spotting scopes, as they are often called. Some birders do use reflector scopes (e.g. Celestron), which offer a fine image at high magnification. They are rather cumbersome, however, and take some getting used to because you see a mirror image and have to pan the scope the 'wrong' way to follow a moving bird.

Like binoculars, scopes have vital statistics that report the magnification (often a range, because many scopes have zoom lenses) and width of the objective lens. Magnification typically is 20x, 30x or 40x for fixed magnifications, and 15–60x for zoom lenses. Because the magnification is much greater, scopes need a larger objective lens, generally 60–80 mm. (As with binoculars, it is a trade-off between weight and image brightness.)

A compact telescope with 45° offset eye-piece

The main decision to be made is what level of magnification you require. Zooms are versatile, but they tend to have a small field of view. As a result, most birders prefer to use a wide-angle lens with a fixed magnification (usually 30x). Most good scopes offer a range of lenses, so if you're really undecided you can always get both zoom and fixed wide-angle lenses. But you'll probably end up not using the zoom much.

You also have to choose between a straight-through eye-piece and an angled eye-piece (typically offset 45°). Again, this is a personal choice. It's easier to locate birds through a straight-through scope, but an angled eye-piece is much more comfortable for protracted use, especially if you're looking at birds above the horizontal (e.g. soaring raptors or forest canopy birds). With practice, it is easy to find birds with an angled eye-piece.

Finally, some standard scopes offer two kinds of lenses: regular and fluorite. Standard lenses scatter more light, resulting in a grey, washed-out image in poor light. Fluorite lenses give a slightly brighter image and offer a marked advantage in poor light, but cost almost twice as much.

In addition to scopes, there are more specialized products. For protracted use, you might consider binocular telescopes, which are basically a huge and very expensive pair of binoculars. Their main advantage is that you can use both eyes. Another relatively low magnification (20x) option is stabilized binoculars, which use a gyroscope to cancel hand-shake. The image quality is impressive in top-of-the-range models, but they are heavy and expensive. A new addition to the market is a small eyepiece that screws onto Swarovski binoculars, turning them into a 20x telescope.

Tripods

Having spent a lot of money on a good scope, the worst thing you can do is to buy a cheap tripod. A poor tripod will kill the pleasure of using a scope. The most important thing is to get a tripod head that is designed for use with video cameras rather than still photography. Ask for tripods with fluid heads and try them out with your scope. The head should pan and tilt smoothly, and not droop under the weight of the scope.

You then have to decide how large and heavy a tripod to buy. The tripod should be tall enough when fully extended to allow you to stand comfortably while looking through your scope (having an angled eyepiece helps). Light tripods are obviously easier to carry, but they are less stable and can be almost useless in a strong wind. One solution is to have a heavy, solid tripod for car-based birding, and a smaller, lightweight model for travel or when walking long distances.

A scope and tripod are not the most convenient things to lug around. You want them ready for use, but you want your hands free at the same time to use your binoculars. Most birders rig up a strap that allows the scope and tripod to be slung over a shoulder. There is also a commercially-available backpack system.

There are alternatives to tripods. Monopods are lighter and are quick to set up, but they don't allow you to relax and really 'soak up' a bird. Stock mounts allow you to use a scope on an unsteady platform such as a ship (you wouldn't want to even try using a scope on a small boat!). Finally, window mounts are available for the serious car-based birder, for attaching a tripod head to the car window. A more low-tech approach is to throw a bean bag or sand bag over the windowsill and use it as a steady base for the scope.

A good, sturdy tripod

A WORD OF ADVICE

- Practise using your new scope. As with binoculars, it takes a bit of practice to locate birds quickly, especially if they're moving. (Raptors overhead in a cloudless sky are a good challenge!)
- If you're using your scope in a strong wind, sit down. Extending the tripod increases wind-shake. Also try to hunker down in the shelter of a rock or bush.
- Never use a scope through a window – the minor blemishes in window glass become overwhelming when magnified through a scope.

Recorders

Like bird photography, top-quality recording is an activity in itself, requiring dedication and specialized equipment. Fortunately, birders can obtain adequate results using relatively cheap, simple gear. Birders' recordings are of immense value to ornithologists, and should be submitted to sound libraries.

Until recently, virtually all birders used standard cassette tape decks in either palm-size or larger format. Reel-to-reel recorders give a better quality recording, but are bulky and heavy, and remain the exclusive domain of professional recorders. There are now two competing digital recording formats: DAT (digital audio tape) and mini-disk (MD). In time, digital recorders with their greater ease of use will probably prevail, but for now standard cassette recorders are the most reliable in the field. Another drawback to most portable DAT and MD players is that they lack a built-in speaker, which means yet another piece of equipment to carry.

Directional versus parabolic microphones

For most purposes, small, hand-held tape recorders are fine for playing taped bird calls. However, their built-in microphones are woefully inadequate for recording birds in the field. This is because they are designed to pick up sounds from all around the microphone. To make useful bird recordings, you need a much more directional microphone.

There are two options: a directional (shotgun) microphone (which has a very sensitive microphone at the end of a long tube) or a parabolic microphone (which uses a dish-like parabola to focus sound from a specific direction onto a microphone).

The size of parabolic microphones makes them unwieldy so most birders opt for a directional microphone. Sennheiser is the industry leader, but many other manufacturers make directional microphones. The Sennheiser MKE300 gives good recordings and is easy to use, although professionals tend to use the larger (and more costly) ME66 or 67. These microphones are relatively small and easy to use, but they are not good for picking up weak calls because there is no magnification of the signal. An electronic amplifier may be used to magnify the signal after it is captured, but it also magnifies any background noise.

With a parabolic microphone, the sound energy from a large area is concentrated, giving much stronger recording signals. The strength of the signal, and the ability to detect low frequencies, increases with the size of the parabola. To be effective, parabolic microphones need to be at least 30 cm across.

A directional microphone and small tape recorder

Most birders use either a walkman-size dictaphone recorder (e.g. Sony TCM 50DV) or a large-format, 'professional' tape deck (e.g. Sony TCM 5000 EV). The latter costs much more, but has a louder speaker and enables you to monitor recordings through headphones and to control recording strength. They also require large-jack microphones, which are better but larger and much more expensive. So you're looking at either a small, compact recorder (must have a microphone socket) and small-jack microphone for about R1 000 to R2 000 or a large-format tape deck and microphone for five or more times the price. If you're taping calls primarily for playback purposes, the quality of the recording is rarely critical – a cheap recorder and a directional microphone are more than adequate.

Making recordings

Making good recordings takes lots of patience, but can be immensely rewarding. Here are a few hints:

- **Don't move while recording.** Directional microphones are extremely sensitive to vibration. Keep still and hold the microphone as steady as possible.
- **Make recordings when you're on your own.** You cannot make good recordings with other people whispering or moving around in the background.
- **Get as close to the bird as possible.** The quality of your recording depends on the signal strength, and this drops dramatically with increasing distance. If necessary, try a short playback to bring the calling bird closer to you.
- **Minimize background noise.** Don't try to record in a noisy environment such as near a road. Try to position yourself relative to the bird so that the amount of background noise is minimal. Streams and waterfalls are especially bad.
- **Avoid wind and rain.** Wind buffets the microphone and can ruin recordings. Reduce its impact by recording downwind, shielding the microphone with your body or a rock or bush, and use a 'shaggy dog' microphone cover (available for more expensive microphones). Recording in the rain is even worse; be sure to shield the microphone from raindrops.
- **Use tape freely.** Blank cassettes are cheap, so don't worry about long silences. These can be edited out later, but you can't recapture a unique call that you miss because the tape wasn't rolling.

Sound libraries

Once you've made some recordings, send them to a sound library to be archived. Magnetic tapes deteriorate with time, but sound libraries store songs digitally. Libraries will ask you to sign an agreement stipulating whether your recordings may be used for research purposes or for commercial use. If they are used commercially, you are entitled to ask for payment. Another incentive to submitting recordings is that some libraries offer major contributors free access to their holdings.

In South Africa, the main sound library is the Percy FitzPatrick Sound Library, Transvaal Museum, PO Box 413, Pretoria 0001 (Tel: 012-322 7632).

Photographing birds

Photographing birds is really a separate activity from birding. Good birders seldom make good bird photographers and vice versa. This is because it takes time and effort to obtain quality photographs, and most birders would rather be out looking at birds! It's nice to have a camera and long lens, if only to document any exciting rarity that you find, but you probably won't want to lug it around with you in the field.

For any serious bird photography, you're going to have to make a significant investment in equipment (lenses alone can cost over R100 000). The type of equipment you select is determined to a large extent by your budget.

- **Cameras.** The basic requirement is a 35 mm SLR (single lens reflex) camera. Larger format cameras give sharper images but cost a lot more, and digital cameras still lack the sharpness of chemical films. Try to get a camera with a quiet shutter action to avoid disturbing birds. Automatic cameras are convenient, but remember to carry spare batteries. The more electronic gizmos you have (e.g. autofocus, motor winder), the more batteries you use, and the more things that can go wrong.
- **Lenses.** Shorter lenses (e.g. 70–200 mm zoom) can be used if photographing a nest from a hide, but for most bird photography you need a good telephoto lens, at least 300 mm or longer. This gives you a level of magnification approaching that of binoculars. To freeze a bird's movement you need fast shutter speeds and a lens that lets in a lot of light (i.e. has a large objective) and has a large aperture option (f 5.6 or less). Bear in mind that depth of field (the range over which objects are in crisp focus) decreases with increasing aperture size. You can boost the magnification of your telephoto lens with teleconverters (1.4–2x), but these further reduce the amount of light reaching the film. Some telescopes offer camera adapters that allow you to use them as a long lens. The quality is generally not great, but it's fine for recording rarities.
- **Flashes.** Flashes allow you to photograph in poor light and to freeze birds in action with very fast shutter speeds (1/1000 second). For most shots you will need more than a built-in flash, and for some shots an array of flashes. Get a flash that is dedicated to your camera to make using it as simple as possible.
- **Film.** Use only slide film if you want to publish your pictures, and use the slowest film that the light level allows (preferably

Ethics in bird photography

Because bird photographers have to get close to birds, they need to be especially careful not to disturb birds. Extra caution is needed when photographing birds at their nests. Resist the temptation to cut back vegetation to expose a nest. Err on the side of caution, and consider your actions very carefully before attempting to photograph endangered birds. Don't photograph at the nests of birds listed 'Not to be disturbed' by the breeding bird survey (p. 85).

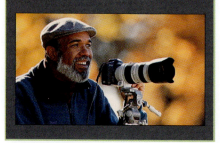

PRACTICAL BIRDING

100 ASA or less) to maximize the sharpness of the image. Remember that slower films need more light, which requires increased exposure and reduces the depth of field.
- **Tripods.** For longer telephoto lenses (anything >300 mm), hand-shake becomes a significant problem. Unless you buy a new, image-stabilized lens (expensive and heavy on batteries), use a tripod, monopod or bean bag (if in a car) to steady the camera. A stock-mount is useful when stalking birds or photographing birds in flight.
- **Video.** Video cameras don't produce publishable images, but they can be very useful for capturing bird behaviour and documenting rarities.

Field techniques

To take good photographs of birds, you have to get close to the birds. There are three basic approaches:

Hides – permanent or self-made – provide ideal cover for photography.

- **Use a hide:** Hides should be as unobtrusive as possible and firmly guyed so that nothing flaps in the wind. To use a hide, you have to be able to predict where a bird will be (e.g. a nest, roost or feeding site). When photographing nesting birds, erect the hide at some distance from the nest, and then slowly move it closer over successive days, checking each time that the birds' behaviour remains the same. For small birds, start at least 3 m from the nest and approach no closer than 1.5 m. Safe approach distances increase for larger birds. It's best to enter the hide when the birds are not around, or ask a friend to accompany you to the hide and then walk away to confuse any birds that may be watching.
- **Use a vehicle:** Cars make good mobile hides. Have your camera ready because you often have only a few seconds to shoot. Approach the birds silently by turning off the engine and rolling closer. Remember to make no sudden movements inside the car.
- **Stalk:** This is when you use your birding field skills to get close to birds. It requires patience, perseverance, and a large film budget, but can yield striking results.

Other birding gadgets

Once you've got all the usual birding paraphernalia, you might consider a GPS (Global Positioning System), which uses satellites to tell you where you are to the nearest 10 m or so. It's great for guiding you back to a specific site, and even more useful if you're atlasing, counting or making nest observations (see 'Making a contribution to ornithology', p. 80).

Another useful gadget is an altimeter. GPS gives an estimate of height, but it's not as accurate as a good altimeter, and it doesn't work well in a forest. Knowing your elevation is useful if you're birding the montane forests of Africa, and even more so in South America. A nice recent development is a hand-held GPS that includes an altimeter.

MAKING A CONTRIBUTION TO ORNITHOLOGY

Malachite Kingfisher being ringed

Thanks to the large number of highly competent amateurs complementing professional ornithologists, birds are the best-known group of animals. However, there is still a lot to be learnt about birds and the many facets of their biology. Amateur birders can make important contributions in many areas, such as making species lists, bird counts, nest reporting and ringing birds. All these activities contribute significantly to bird conservation.

It is important to stay alert. Report unusual occurrences to your local bird club newsletter or chat group. Be particularly alert to the disappearance of species from an area – this is much easier to overlook than range expansions.

Atlasing and counting

Atlasing (compiling species lists to map the distributions of birds) is, perhaps, the most basic contribution a birder can make. Amateur birders provided the vast majority of records for *The Atlas of Southern African Birds*, a massive, two-volume work published in 1997 by BirdLife South Africa, that maps the distribution of all southern Africa's birds. Indeed, atlasing became the driving force behind many birders' outings in southern Africa in the 1980s and 1990s, and was responsible for many people's interest in birds and their competence at identifying them.

A new southern African bird atlas is being considered. This may seem like overkill, but a comparison of bird distribution in southern Africa in the 1980s and 1990s with bird distribution ten years hence will be invaluable when assessing changes in the conservation status of birds and in the broader environment.

In the meantime, there are various projects on the go: The Birds in Reserves Project (BIRP) needs bird lists for all South African protected areas, and – for a more quantitative assessment of the status of bird populations – there are two bird-count projects that currently focus on larger bird species: Co-ordinated Waterbird Counts (CWAC) counts water birds twice a year at wetlands throughout the country and Co-ordinated Avifaunal Roadcounts (CAR) monitors populations of large terrestrial birds by twice-yearly counts along fixed road routes.

Further information on these projects and their requirements may be obtained from the Avian Demography Unit (ADU) or your local BirdLife-affiliated bird club. (For addresses, see p. 90–91.) Contributors to any of the ADU projects receive *Bird Numbers*, an informative journal that gives feedback on amateur birding projects.

Watching nesting birds

Observing birds at their nests and following the development of a brood of chicks are among the most rewarding activities that birding offers. It is also a very important source of information about the natural history of birds.

The breeding biology of many southern African birds is little known. You can make an important contribution through careful observation of breeding behaviour – which bird (male, female or both) builds the nest, how many eggs are laid, which bird incubates the eggs and for how long, the length of time the eggs take to hatch, whether the young are brooded and, if so, for how long and by which bird, the presence of helpers at the nest, which bird

African Paradise Flycatcher

feeds the chicks and when the chicks leave the nest. It will not always be feasible, however, to collect all of this information, and the paramount concern must be for the breeding birds. Some birds abandon breeding attempts when disturbed.

Estimates of breeding success may be made on the basis of repeated observations of nest contents, providing important information about the health of bird populations. Successful reproduction is an essential balance to mortality in bird populations. By measuring breeding success, we get advance warning of the effect of any modification of the environment. If we waited until the impact of change was visible in the population of adult birds, it might well be too late to do anything about it.

BirdLife South Africa has a Nest Record Card Scheme (NERCS) run by the Avian Demography Unit to capture breeding observations and monitor breeding success for bird species in southern Africa. Their most important requirement (other than that you avoid undue disturbance) is that you make sure you identify the bird species correctly! If you are keen to contribute information to the Nest Record Card Scheme, contact the ADU or your local BirdLife-affiliated bird club (see pp. 90–91). They will supply a booklet that outlines the do's and don'ts of nest finding and observing.

Finding nests

Like bird identification, finding birds' nests takes practice and patience. You can boost your chances of success by searching in the right season (spring-summer for most species, although many species can breed virtually throughout the year). Changes in a bird's

Egg collecting

In the past, many good birders started off by collecting eggs. Indeed, some people are obsessed with eggs, and see birds only as an intermediate step in the egg-making process. Nowadays, egg collecting is rightly frowned upon, and it is illegal to own a collection of birds' eggs. Birds have enough problems to survive in the modern world without the additional burden of having their eggs stolen every time they lay a clutch. Of course, collecting the odd clutch will make very little difference to many species, but the problem is that collectors value the eggs of rare species simply because they are rare. This leads to a vicious cycle of increasing rarity and eventual extinction – witness the demise of the Great Auk, where the last birds were killed because of the high price put on their skins by museums.

Collecting things is a phase that many children go through. You can divert this urge into searching for nests and recording what happens to them (a benefit both to ornithology and the budding ornithologist). Learning how to find nests at an early age imparts skills that are hard to acquire later in life! If the acquisitive urge persists, try redirecting it into less destructive outlets such as collecting the skulls and feet of dead birds or a bird-ringing apprenticeship.

Greater Kestrel egg

behaviour are the most important clue that it is breeding. Experienced nesters can tell at a glance if a bird is likely to be nesting or not, simply by the way it behaves. Lesser mortals will have to look for birds carrying nesting material or food, and then watch from a discreet distance to see where they go. Breeding birds are often quite cautious, and if you are too close to them or their nest, they won't go to the nest. You may also see passerines and woodpeckers carrying white, globular objects. These are the chicks' faecal sacs, which the parents remove from the nest, so watch to see where they go after dumping the sacs, and listen for the calls of hungry chicks.

Knysna Woodpecker

Once you have identified the location of the nest as accurately as possible (ideally from several angles), approach the site, and very cautiously look for the nest. It helps to know where the nest is likely to be (e.g. on the ground or in a bush) and what it's likely to look like (e.g. a hole, an open cup, a dome). *Roberts' Birds of Southern Africa* summarizes this information. Even if you are armed with such knowledge, however, nests can be remarkably well hidden. If you don't find the nest immediately – some birds are quite sneaky, landing some distance from where they want to go – back off and try watching from another vantage. If you persist in looking when you're not absolutely sure where the nest is, you run the very real risk of accidentally destroying the nest.

Nests in different microhabitats are found in different ways. Tell-tale splashes of fresh droppings may give away the whereabouts of cliff nests. Ground-nesting birds often flush from the nest when you're almost on top of them. It's worth

Tools of the trade

Not all nests are conveniently located for inspection of their contents. Many are high up in trees, or in burrows or holes.

Some inaccessible nests can be examined by using an angled mirror on the end of a long pole. Carefully position the mirror over the nest and then examine the reflected nest contents through binoculars. Nests up to 20 m above ground can be inspected in this way without disturbing the birds as much as you would if you climbed up yourself or used a ladder.

Hole nests pose another challenge. Nests with straight entrances can be inspected with a torch, or by reflecting sunlight into the hole using a small mirror or even a watch face. Nests with angled entrances can be inspected by lowering a torch bulb attached by loose wires to a battery into the hole, and then using a mirror on a flexible piece of wire to see the nest contents.

checking for a nest when a bird flushes from your feet. Many ground nesters use distraction displays to lure you away from their nests. Stand back and watch where the bird goes. Some species also use the same nest in successive breeding attempts, so check old sites for signs of fresh activity.

Once you've found a nest, inspect the contents, record the information in your notebook or directly onto a nest record card, and then leave the area as quickly as possible. Make sure that you can find the nest again – breeding success can only be estimated if you visit a nest more than once. Mark the general area in some way, for instance by knotting a piece of grass near the nest; otherwise, you may waste a lot of time rediscovering nests.

Human intrusion

An overriding concern when studying breeding birds is the extent to which the observer affects the behaviour of the birds and the likelihood of breeding success. You often hear people say that you shouldn't touch eggs or chicks, because the parent bird will be able to smell/sense the intrusion, and will abandon the nest. This is a good story for the public because it helps to keep untrained fingers where they belong, but it is only a story. Nevertheless, you do have to be very careful in the early stages of nest construction and egg laying because birds are more likely to quit at this stage, when they have a relatively small investment in the breeding attempt. Also, some species are more sensitive than others to disturbance, so err on the side of caution.

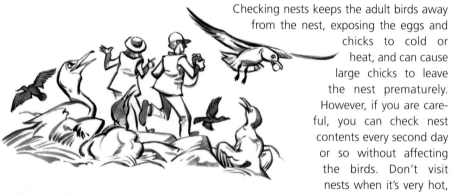

Checking nests keeps the adult birds away from the nest, exposing the eggs and chicks to cold or heat, and can cause large chicks to leave the nest prematurely. However, if you are careful, you can check nest contents every second day or so without affecting the birds. Don't visit nests when it's very hot, cold or windy, and don't remain near a nest for long. Only one person should approach a nest each time it's checked, and the nest should always be approached from the same direction to reduce damage to surrounding vegetation. If you want to make protracted observations of a nest (e.g. to see how often chicks are fed, and by whom), you need to build a hide or remain at a sufficient distance so as not to alter the behaviour of the birds. (see 'Photographing birds', p. 78).

You have to be especially careful when visiting breeding colonies, because predators such as gulls or ibises can use the opportunity to steal eggs and chicks. Also, chicks may wander away from the nest during the confusion of your visit, and may then be persecuted by adults from other nests in the colony. As a rule, you should avoid entering bird colonies, and remain far enough away that adult birds are not flushed from their nests.

Some threatened and sensitive species should not be disturbed while breeding. The Nest Record Card Scheme (NERCS) lists the following:

African Penguin	Great White Pelican
Yellow-breasted Pipit	Marabou Stork
Bald Ibis	Cape Vulture
Bat Hawk	Palmnut Vulture
Taita Falcon	Wattled Crane
Caspian Tern	Rudd's Lark
Botha's Lark	Blue Swallow
Pink-backed Pelican (*left*)	

Ringing birds

Ringing or banding birds is another very interesting and rewarding activity that contributes to our understanding of bird biology. Ringing birds provides information on movements and survival, and also on moult and morphology (the mass and size of birds). You have to undergo intensive training as an apprentice ringer before you can get a permit to ring birds by yourself. If you are keen to see whether ringing is your thing, most bird clubs have licensed ringers who are more than happy to take along volunteers. SAFRING runs training courses for ringers in most years (*see* 'Ornithological Institutes, p. 93).

Catching birds

The first thing to do when ringing is to catch the birds, which is not always easy. The most frequent technique is to use mist nets, very fine nets that are almost invisible once they are erected. Birds in forests and woodlands fail to see the nets and get caught when they try to fly through the nets. The art of netting is to know where to put nets and to get them up at the right time (by dawn is ideal). Mist netting doesn't work very well in open habitats, because the nets are more visible and birds generally avoid them. For some birds like waders, you can get around this problem by setting nets at night.

You can also shoot nets over birds on the ground, using either explosive charges (cannon nets) or elastic cords (clap nets). The latter are useful for catching garden birds when they are feeding sites on the ground.

A Reed Warbler caught in a mist net

Another technique is to use baited walk-in traps or even to place a walk-in trap over a bird's nest. Raptors are best caught using balchatri traps, which are a series of fine monofilament loops attached to a cage containing a mouse or similar tasty raptor snack. When the raptor tries to catch the mouse, it gets tangled in the loops, and the mouse escapes unscathed (unless it has a weak heart!). There are many other, even more exotic ways to catch birds, such as the 'dazzle and gong' technique or 'war-whooping', but limited space precludes describing them here.

Again, irrespective of the method used to catch birds, a ringer's primary concern is for the well-being of the birds. Every effort must be made to ensure that capture and subsequent ringing has no short- or long-term impact.

Reporting ringed birds

If you find a dead bird that is ringed, report it to SAFRING (University of Cape Town, Rondebosch, 7701; Ph 021 650-2421). Rings supplied by SAFRING are stamped 'Inform SAFRING, UCT'. (old rings read 'Inform Zoo Pretoria'.) Rings from other parts of the world have a different message, but you should still report them to SAFRING, who will contact the relevant ringing organization.

You need to report the ring number, type of bird (if you know what it is), the date and place found, and cause of death (if known) together with your contact details. It's best to send the ring with the report, but if you don't, make sure you get the number right! Whenever you report a ringed bird to SAFRING, they will tell you when the bird was ringed, at what age, and how far it had moved.

You might also see ringed birds while you're birding. If you can read the ring number (this is possible for large rings like penguin flipper rings), report it to SAFRING, supplying the species, date, place and the bird's activity (stress that it was not dead!). If the ring is coloured with a number stencilled into it, report the colour of the number and ring as well as the number (e.g. black A69 on a yellow ring). There's no point reporting ringed birds where you can't read the number, but if the bird has unmarked colour rings, note the exact combination and report it to SAFRING.

You need to give the arrangement of all rings for each leg in order to identify the individual: e.g. red over green on the left leg, blue over metal on the right leg. Sometimes birds are marked in other ways – nasal tags, neck rings, patagial tags (through the wing) and dye marks (generally yellow or pink) – so that they can be identified in the field. Once again, SAFRING should be able to find out where they are from, and will inform the relevant researcher.

Measuring birds

Field guides typically give a total length and perhaps a wingspan estimate to convey the size of each species, but these measures are rather crude. To assess whether females are bigger than males, or species A is bigger than species B, you have to take much more precise measurements. The standard measurements taken (and summarized in handbooks such as Roberts' Birds) are: wing, tail, tarsus and bill length. Other useful measures include total head length, bill depth and bill width. Sometimes several measures of bill length are taken because the standard measure from the start of the feathers to the tip changes with moult and wear.

Total head length of a Malachite Kingfisher

Processing birds

Once the bird is caught, it is placed in a cloth bird bag or holding box, where it can remain cool and calm until it is processed. Most birds are weighed, measured (see 'Measuring birds'), examined for moult, aged and sexed (if possible), and then fitted with a uniquely numbered ring, typically around the bird's leg. These rings are designed to last the lifetime of the bird, and have no impact on the bird's survival. In some studies, birds also receive colour rings that allow recognition of individual birds or cohorts without recapture.

An essential part of any successful ringing programme is careful data management. In southern Africa, SAFRING provides rings and other ringing equipment, collates ringing information, and provides feedback to people who find ringed birds.

Birds in the hand

Dead birds

Occasionally, you come across dead birds, often road-kills or birds that have died after colliding with windows. These birds are useful for scientific study, and can prevent the deaths of other birds that would otherwise have to be collected for research purposes. If the bird is freshly dead, seal it in a plastic bag or a suitable container (ice-cream and margarine tubs are ideal for smaller birds that might get damaged) and freeze it as soon as possible. Remember to include a label (in pencil) with the bird, giving the place collected, the date found, the cause of death (if known) and your name and contact details. This is very important – specimens without collection details have to be discarded. Then deliver the frozen bird to your local museum. If you live far from a museum, but have an especially interesting specimen, give the museum a call to see if they can arrange to collect it from you.

What if the bird is not freshly dead? Inspect it for bird rings, and if it is banded report the ring number to SAFRING (*see* 'Reporting ringed birds', p. 86) along with the location, date and cause of death (if known); estimate how long the bird has been dead (is it days, weeks or months?). Try to identify the bird. If it's a rare or unusual bird and is still intact, it may be of value for its skeleton or feathers. Seal the body in a plastic bag, label it, and contact your local museum to check if it wants the specimen. The more experienced birder may also glean useful information on moult from dead birds (*see* box on 'Scoring moult').

Very occasionally, a large number of dead birds may be found together – the result, possibly, of an exceptional cold spell, an outbreak of disease, natural toxins such as botulism, or a hail storm, or even deliberate action such as poisoning. Seabirds also are prone to occasional 'wrecks' when large numbers come ashore (dead and/or alive). Mass mortality is worth reporting to your local conservation agency as well as to the local bird club, museum or ornithological institute. Remember to check all birds for rings.

Scoring moult

Feathers slowly abrade, and thus have to be replaced every year or so. Old feathers are dropped and new feathers emerge in a bluish sheath, which splits to expose the new feather. The following scoring system is widely used:

0 = old feather
1 = new feather still entirely in its sheath (termed a 'pin')
2 = feather has emerged from the sheath, but vane has not opened
3 = vane formed, but feather less than half its full length
4 = growing feather more than half its full length
5 = new, fully formed feather (with no sign of blue sheath at base)

Ornithologists focus most attention on the replacement of flight feathers, especially the outer wing feathers or primaries. These are scored from the inner primary (P1) to the outer primary (usually P10). Waves of moult typically proceed regularly from inner to outer primaries, but large birds may have more complex moult patterns.

A moult database is kept by the Avian Demographic Unit (University of Cape Town).

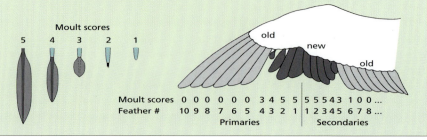

PRACTICAL BIRDING

Injured birds and 'abandoned' nestlings

What should you do if you find an injured bird?

If the bird is simply entangled in fishing line, and looks to be in good health (i.e. puts up a good fight when you try to catch it), disentangle the bird and release it. Similarly, if a bird is stunned after flying into a window, release it once it recovers. However, in other circumstances, as when the bird has broken bones or oiled plumage, professional help is necessary. Catch the bird, using a net if needs be. If it's a large bird, don gloves and throw a sheet over it to avoid getting bitten, clawed or battered by its wings. Then place it in a sufficiently large, well-ventilated box, with an absorbent lining such as old newspaper. Keep the bird in the dark to reduce stress, and transport it to your nearest rehabilitation centre (see 'Addresses and other useful information', p. 90).

It is illegal to keep wild birds without a permit. Rehabilitation centres have such permits, and they are in the best position to assess the likelihood of an injured bird recovering to the point where it can be released into the wild. If this is not the case, and the bird is not sufficiently rare to warrant inclusion in a captive-breeding programme, the bird may have to be euthanased.

You might also encounter seemingly abandoned nestlings. Before you do anything else, assess the age and state of development of the chick. Many ground-nesting species have precocial chicks that can run or swim from birth, and can forage for themselves. It's best to leave such chicks alone, unless they are injured or are in a dangerous situation (e.g. in the middle of a road). If the chick is in danger, move it to a nearby suitable habitat and leave it to fend for itself. Similarly, if the chick is fully feathered and can flutter, it has probably left the nest already and can be left alone or, if necessary, moved a few metres to a more secure site. Doves often continue to feed chicks that fall out of their flimsy nests.

If you find an altricial chick – one that is born naked and blind, and is totally dependent on its parents for food – it does need help (unless you're prepared to let nature take its course). The best course of action is to find the chick's nest and return it to the nest. Such chicks cannot move far, so the nest should be in the vicinity. If you can't find the nest, but the parents are present (they will be acting in an agitated manner), try putting the chick in a suitable artificial nest. Only as a last resort should you take the chick to a rehabilitation centre. If you do, remember to keep the chick warm and dry.

A wounded raptor

ADDRESSES AND OTHER USEFUL INFORMATION

Bird Clubs

South African bird clubs
BirdLife South Africa
(PO Box 515, Randburg 2125.
Tel. 011-789 1122;
www.birdlife.org.za) is a federation of 24 bird clubs in South Africa, (denoted *) with a further 15 affiliate clubs. Contact BirdLife SA for details of your nearest bird club.

Eastern Cape
* BirdLife Eastern Cape,
  PO Box 27454, Greenacres 6057
Diaz Cross Bird Club,
  3 Florence St.,
  Grahamstown 6140
* Border Bird Club,
  PO Box 2440,
  Beacon Bay 5205

Free State
* Free State Bird Club,
  PO Box 6614,
  Bloemfontein 9300
Goldfields Bird Club,
  PO Box 580,
  Virginia 9430
* Riemland Bird Club,
  PO Box 2270,
  Sasolburg 9570
* Memel Bird Club,
  PO Box 282, Memel 2970

* Vaal Dam Bird Club,
  PO Box 7, Deneysville 9412

Gauteng
* Witwatersrand Bird Club,
  PO Box 72091,
  Parkview 2122
* Inkwasi Bird Club,
  PO Box 588,
  Gallo Manor 2052
* Rand Barbet Bird Club,
  PO Box 261, Rivonia 2074
* Sandton Bird Club,
  PO Box 650890,
  Benmore 2010
* President Ridge Bird Club,
  PO Box 3049,
  Cramer View 2060
* Pretoria Bird Club,
  PO Box 12563,
  Hatfield 0028
First Encounters,
  PO Box 84648,
  Greenside, 2034
Johannesburg Country Club Bird Club, PO Box 467, Rivonia 2128

Kwa-Zulu Natal
* Natal Bird Club,
  PO Box 1218,
  Durban 4000
* Natal Midlands Bird Club,
  PO Box 2772,
  Pietermaritzburg 3200

* BirdLife Northern Natal,
  PO Box 20421,
  Newcastle, 2940
* South Coast Trogons,
  PO Box 45160,
  Port Shepstone 4240
Mtubatuba Bird Club,
  PO Box 286,
  Mtubatuba 3935

Mpumalanga
* Lowveld Bird Club,
  PO Box 19334,
  Nelspruit 1200
Grassveld Bird Club,
  PO Box 5262,
  Secunda, 2302
Middelburg Bird Club,
  PO Box 13324,
  Dennesig 1050
Witbank Bird Club,
  PO Box 6173,
  Witbank 1040

North-West
* Rustenburg Bird Club,
  PO Box 3021,
  Rustenburg 0300
* Wesvaal Bird Club,
  PO Box 6098,
  Flamberg 2572
Vaal Reefs Bird Club,
  PO Box 5129,
  Vaal Reefs 2621

Northern Province
- Pietersburg Bird Club,
  PO Box 31086,
  Superbia 0759
- Soutpansberg Bird Club,
  PO Box 737, Louis Trichardt 0920
- Phalaborwa Bird Club,
  PO Box 76, Phalaborwa 1390

Tzaneen Bird Club,
  PO Box 40, Tzaneen 0850

Western Cape
- Cape Bird Club, PO Box 5022,
  Cape Town 8000

Tygerberg Bird Club, PO Box 36,
  Durbanville 7551
Somerset West Bird Club,
  PO Box 1558, Somerset West 7130
Robertson Bird Club, PO Box 164,
  Robertson 6705
- Rein's Coastal Nature Reserve Bird Club,
  PO Box 298, Albertinia 6645

The Lakes Bird Club,
  PO Box 792,
  Sedgefield 6573
Plett Bird Club, PO Box 268,
  Plettenberg Bay 6600
William Quentin Karoo Bird Club,
  PO Box 140, Beaufort West 6970

Other Bird clubs

African Bird Club, c/o BirdLife International,
  Wellbrook Court, Girton Road, Cambridge
  CB3 0NA, UK; www.africanbirdclub.org
  (journal: *Bulletin of the African Bird Club*)
Botswana Bird Club, PO Box 71, Gaberone,
  Botswana (journal: *Babbler*)
Clube Ornitologico de Mocambique,
  Museu de Historia Natural – UEM,
  PO Box 257, Maputo, Mozambique;
  email: com@natural.uem.mz
Namibia Bird Club, PO Box 67, Windhoek,
  Namibia (journal: *Lanioturdus*)

Swaziland Bird Club, c/o Ara Monadjem, Dept
  of Biological Sciences, University of
  Swaziland, PO Box 4, Kwaluseni, Swaziland;
  email: *ara@science.uniswa.sz*
BirdLife Zimbabwe, PO Box CY160,
  Causeway, Harare, Zimbabwe;
  e-mail: *birds@zol.co.zw*
  (journal: *Honeyguide*)

Guides and other books

Where-to-watch site guides for southern Africa

Bird checklists of KwaZulu-Natal reserves.
  Part 1: The Greater Durban Area,
  R. Cowgill & S. Davis, Mondi BirdLife
  South Africa Guide 21, 1998.
Birding in southern KwaZulu-Natal,
  D. G. Allan, Margate: Hisbiscus Coast and
  Country Publicity Association, 1998.
Birds of the south-western Cape and Where to Watch Them, W. Petersen & M. Tripp,
  Mondi Southern Birds 20, 1995.
Essential Birding: Western South Africa,
  C. Cohen & C. Spottiswoode, Struik,
  Cape Town, 2000.
Go Birding in the Transvaal,
  B. Ryan & J. Isom. Struik,
  Cape Town, 1990.
Top Birding Spots in Southern Africa,
  H. Chittendon, Southern Books,
  Halfway House, 1992.
Where to See Birds in KwaZulu-Natal,
  G. Bennett & S. Herbert,
  Mondi Southern Birds 19, 1995.
Where to Watch Birds in Southern Africa,
  A. Berruti & J. C. Sinclair, Struik,
  Cape Town, 1983.

Useful books

Attracting Birds to your Garden, R. Trendler & L. Hes, Struik, Cape Town, 1994.
Birds of Africa (vol 6. and counting), Keith, Fry & Urban (eds), Academic Press, London.
Handbook of the Birds of the World (vol 6. and counting), J. del Hoyo, A. Elliott & J. Sargatal (eds), Lynx Edicions, Barcelona.
Nesting Birds: the Breeding Habits of Southern African Birds, P. Steyn, Fernwood Press, Vlaeberg, 1996.
The Atlas of Southern African Birds (vol 2.), J. A. Harrison et al. (eds), BirdLife South Africa, Johannesburg, 1997.

Book suppliers

If your bird club and local bookshop don't stock a book you want, try:
Russel Friedman, PO Box 73, Halfway House 1685; fax: 011-702 1403; tel: 011-702 2300/1; email: *rfbooks@iafrica.com*;
or shop via the web:
www.amazon.com,
www.amazon.co.uk,
www.nhbs.com

Guides and trip reports for other parts of the world

The Foreign Bird Reports and Information Service, 6 Skipton Crescent, Berkeley Pendesham, Worcester WR4 0LG, United Kingdom
Where to watch birds in Africa, N. Wheatley, Russel Friedman, Halfway House, 1995.
Where to watch birds in Asia. N. Wheatley, Christopher Helm, London, 1996.
Where to watch birds in South America, N. Wheatley, Christopher Helm, London, 1994.
www.bsc-eoc.org/links/ accesses more than 6 000 trip reports, searchable by country or region.
www.camacdonald.com/birding/ is a useful summary of regional birding information.

Birders viewing seabirds in flight

Websites

There are literally hundreds of birding websites, many of which have links to other sites. The following should get you surfing painlessly:
www.birding.com, a US-based site that has many useful links
www.birding-africa.com, another useful site with a focus on Africa and mystery bird photos
www.bsc-eoc.org/links/ provides country-by-country info, as well as regional links
www.fatbirding.com, perhaps the top UK-based site
www.ornith.cornell.edu/BRP/ links to sonogram software for various computer platforms
www.sabirding.co.za, one of the main South African birding sites
www.surfbirds.com, an international site with growing popularity
www.thayerbirding.com, the leading birding software company
www.wildsounds.co.uk supplies recording equipment
www.zestforbirds.co.za offers SA rarity photos, Cape pelagic trips and SA lists

Rare bird alert

Subscribe by sending a blank message to:
 sararebirdalert-subscribe@egroups.com.
Send sightings to:
 sararebirdalert@egroups.com

Ornithological institutes

Avian Demography Unit and SAFRING,
 University of Cape Town, Rondebosch 7701;
 www.uct.ac.za/depts/stats/adu
Percy FitzPatrick Institute of African
 Ornithology, University of Cape Town,
 Rondebosch 7701;
 www.uct.ac.za/depts/fitzpatrick

Specialist groups

African Raptor Information Centre,
 PO Box 4035, Halfway House 1685
Raptor Conservation Group, PO Box 72155,
 Parkview 2122
 (journal: *Journal of African Raptor Biology*)
African Seabird Group, PO Box 341113,
 Rhodes Gift 7707;
 email: jcooper@botzoo.uct.ac.za
 (journal: *Marine Ornithology*)
Southern African Crane Foundation,
 PO Box 2310, Durban 4000
Vulture Study Group, PO Box 72334,
 Parkview 2122
 (journal: *Vulture News*)

Rehabilitation Centres

Wildcare (previously ARC), PO Box 15121,
 Lynn East 0039,
 tel: (012) 808 1106
Centre for Rehabilitation of Wildlife (CROW)
 PO Box 53007, Yellowwood Park,
 Durban 4011,
 tel: (031) 462 1127

South African National Council for the
 Conservation of Coastal Birds (SANCCOB)
 PO Box 11116, Bloubergrant 7443
 tel: (021) 557 6155

Museums

Bulawayo Museum, PO Box 240, Bulawayo
 (Audrey Msimanga);
 tel: 09263-3-64019;
 e-mail: orni@telconet.co.za
Durban Museum, PO Box 4085, Durban 4000
 (David Allan); tel: 031-311 2247;
 e-mail: david@durban.gov.za
East London Museum, 319 Oxford St.,
 East London 5201 (Carl Vernon);
 tel: 0431-430 686;
 e-mail: elmuseum@mymail.net4u.co.za
McGregor Museum, Kimberley, PO Box 316,
 Kimberley 3800 (Corne Anderson);
 tel: 053-842 0099;
 e-mail: corne@museumsnc.co.za
National Museum, Bloemfontein,
 PO Box 266, Bloemfontein 9300
 (Rick Nuttall); tel: 051-447 9609;
 e-mail: ornito@nasmus.co.za
South African Museum, PO Box 61,
 Cape Town 8000 (Denise Drinkrow);
 tel: 021-424 3330;
 e-mail: ddrinkrow@samuseum.ac.za
State Museum of Namibia,
 PO Box 1203, Windhoek;
 tel: 09264-61-229 808.
Transvaal Museum, Pretoria, PO Box 413,
 Pretoria 0001 (Tamar Cassidy);
 tel: 012-322 7632;
 e-mail: cass-t@nfi.co.za

NEW CLASSIFICATION OF BIRDS

After almost half a century of relative stability in bird classification, major changes have resulted from the use of genetic information to infer evolutionary relationships. The new sequence proposed by Charles Sibley and Jon Ahlquist is gaining growing support. One of its strengths is that it makes sense of the bewildering variety of passerines, where attempts to infer relationships based on bird structure are confounded by convergent evolution (i.e. where birds look the same simply because they live in similar habitats, not because they are closely related). The following table demonstrates how southern African birds are classified under the Sibley & Ahlquist system.

Order (Suborder)	Family	Subfamily	Common name
Struthioniformes	Struthionidae		Ostriches
Galliformes	Phasianidae		Francolins, quails
	Numididae		Guineafowl
Anseriformes	Dendrocygnidae		Whistling ducks
	Anatidae	Oxyurinae	Stiff-tailed ducks
		Anatinae	Typical ducks & geese
Turniciformes	Turnicidae		Buttonquails
Piciformes	Indicatoridae		Honeyguides
	Picidae		Woodpeckers
	Lybiidae		African barbets
Bucerotiformes	Bucerotidae		Typical hornbills
	Bucorvidae		Ground hornbills
Upupiformes	Upupidae		Hoopoes
	Phoeniculidae		Woodhoopoes
	Rhinopomastidae		Scimitarbills
Trogoniformes	Trogonidae		Trogons
Coraciiformes	Coraciidae		Typical rollers
	Alcedinidae		Malachite & related kingfishers
	Dacelonidae		Halcyon & related kingfishers
	Cerylidae		Pied & Giant Kingfishers
	Meropidae		Bee-eaters
Coliiformes	Coliidae		Mousebirds
Cuculiformes	Cuculidae		Old World cuckoos
	Centropidae		Coucals
Psittaciformes	Psittacidae		Parrots & lovebirds
Apodiformes	Apodidae		Swifts
Musophagiformes	Musophagidae		Turacos (loeries)
Strigiformes	Tytonidae		Barn & Grass Owls
	Strigidae		Typical owls
	Caprimulgidae		Nightjars
Columbiformes	Columbidae		Pigeons & doves
Gruiformes	Otididae		Bustards & korhaans
	Gruidae	Balearicinae	Crowned cranes
		Gruinae	Typical cranes
	Rallidae		Rails, crakes, coots
Ciconiiformes (Charadrii)	Pteroclidae		Sandgrouse
	Scolopacidae	Scolopacinae	Snipes, small sandpipers
		Triginae	Large sandpipers
	Rostratulidae		Painted Snipe

Ciconiiformes (Charadrii) **(cont.)**	Jacanidae		Jacanas
	Chionididae		Sheathbills
	Burhinidae		Thick-knees (dikkops)
	Charadriidae	Recurvirostrinae	Oystercatchers, avocets & stilts
		Charadriinae	Plovers & lapwings
	Glareolidae	Dromadinae	Crab Plover
		Glareolinae	Coursers & pratincoles
	Laridae	Larinae	Skuas, gulls & terns
	Accipitridae	Pandioninae	Osprey
		Accipitrinae	Typical raptors
	Sagittaridae		Secretarybird
	Falconidae		Falcons
(Ciconii)	Podicipedidae		Grebes
	Phaethontidae		Tropicbirds
	Sulidae		Gannets & boobies
	Anhingidae		Darters
	Phalacrocoracidae		Cormorants
	Ardeidae		Herons, egrets & bitterns
	Scopidae		Hamerkop
	Phoenicopteridae		Flamingos
	Threskiornitidae		Ibises & spoonbills
	Pelecanidae	Balaenicipitinae	Shoebill
		Pelecaninae	Pelicans
	Ciconiidae	Ciconiinae	Storks
	Fregatidae		Frigatebirds
	Spheniscidae		Penguins
	Procellariidae	Procellariinae	Petrels & shearwaters
		Diomedeinae	Albatrosses
		Hydrobatinae	Storm petrels
Passeriformes (Tyranni)	Pittidae		Pittas
	Eurylaimidae		Broadbills
(Passeri – Corvida)	Laniidae		True shrikes
	Corvidae	Corvinae	Crows, orioles & cuckooshrikes
		Dicrurinae	Drongos, monarch & paradise flycatchers
		Malaconotinae	Bush shrikes, batises & wattle-eyes
(Passeri – Passerida)	Muscicapidae	Turdinae	Thrushes
		Muscicapinae	Chats & Old World flycatchers
	Sturnidae		Starlings
	Certhiidae	Certhiinae	Treecreepers
	Paridae	Remizinae	Penduline tits
		Parinae	Typical tits
	Hirundinidae	Hirundininae	Swallows & martins
	Pycnonotidae		Bulbuls
	Cisticolidae		Cisticolas, prinias, apalises, camaropteras
	Zosteropidae		White-eyes
	Sylviidae	Acrocephalinae	Reed & leaf warblers
		Sylviinae	Typical warblers, babblers, etc.
	Alaudidae		Larks
	Nectariniidae	Promeropinae	Sugarbirds
		Nectariniinae	Sunbirds
	Passeridae	Passerinae	Old World sparrows
		Motacillinae	Wagtails, pipits & longclaws
		Ploceinae	Weavers, widowbirds, bishops, Cukoo Finch
		Estrildinae	Waxbills, firefinches, whydahs, indigobirds
	Fringillidae	Fringillinae	Canaries, seedeaters, siskins & Chaffinch
		Emberizinae	Buntings

NEW CLASSIFICATION OF BIRDS

INDEX

Page references in *italics* indicate illustrations

atlasing 81
attracting birds 35-37
Avian Demography Unit (ADU) 81, 82
banding *see* ringing
big days 64-65
bills *20*
binoculars 9-13, *10, 12, 13,* 74-75
bird clubs 63, 90-91
birding
   at night 38-39
   on foot 33-34
   from vehicle 31-32
   seabirding 39-42
birding sites
   bushveld 49
   coastal 60
   desert 57
   forest 50
   fynbos 54
   grasslands 52
   Karoo 55
   wetlands 58
Birdlife South Africa 63, 81, 82
books 14-15, 91-92
breeding behaviour *see* nesting birds
bushveld 48-49, *49*
calls 26, 28-30, 35-36
cats 45
chat groups 66
chicks 89
classification 18, 20, 27
   new proposed classification 94-95
coastline 59-60, *60*
coloration 21
   abnormalities 69-70, 71, *71*
   colour morphs 25

conservation 80, 81, 85
counting birds 81
dead birds 65, 66, 86, 87-88
description of bird 17-19
desert 56-57, *56, 57*
eggs 82
endemic species
   bushveld 49
   coastal 60, *60*
   desert 57, *57*
   forest 50-51, *51*
   fynbos 54, *54*
   grasslands 52-53, *52*
   Karoo 56, *56*
   wetlands 59, *59*
equipment 9-15, 74-77
estuaries 59-60, *60*
ethics 5, 36, 65-66, 78
feeders 46
feet *20*
field guides 14-15, 61, 70, 91-92
food 37, 45
forest 50-51, *50, 51*
fynbos 53-54
gardens 44-46, *44, 45*
Global Positioning System (GPS) 79
grasslands 51-53, *51, 52*
guides 14-15, 91-92
habitats 17, 43-61
hides 63, 79, *79*
hybridization 70

identification 16-30
   problems 68-70, *68, 69, 70*
injured birds 89
islands 59-60, *60*
jargon 5
jizz 25-26, *25, 69, 69*
Karoo 55-56, *55*
listing 64-66
local birding spots 47
marsh bashing 34
measuring techniques 87, *87*
microphones 76, *76*
mimicry 28, 29
mist nets 66, 85, *85*
moult 23, *68, 69,* 88, *88*
museums 93
names *see* classification
national parks 37
nest boxes 46
nesting birds 46, 81-85, *81, 83, 85*
Nest Record Card Scheme (NERCS) 82, 85
night birding 38-39
note books 15
ornithological institutes 93
parts of bird 17, 19, *19*
photography 78-79
pishing 36
plumage 68-69, *68*
   age differences 22-23, *22, 23*
   colour morphs 25
   moult 23, *68, 69,* 88, *88*
   regional differences 24-25, *24*

plumage (**cont.**)
   seasonal differences 24, *24*
   sex differences 23-24
   pollen staining 70, *70*
Rare Bird Alert 93
rarities 70-71, 73
recorders 76-77
recordings of song 28
   making recordings 77
   using recordings 28, 35-36
   managing tapes 36
rehabilitation centres 93
ringing *80,* 85-87, *86, 87,* 88
seabirding 39-42, *40, 42*
Sibley sequence 94-95
sketching 17-18
song 26, 28-30, 35-36
sonograms 30
sound libraries 77
splits and lumps 72
spotlights 38
squeaking 36
tapes *see* recordings
taxonomy *see* classification
telescopes 74-75, *74*
ticking 65-66
tripods 75, *75,* 79
trip reports 61, 92
vagrants 71, 73
vehicles 31-32, 37, 79
websites 64, 92
wetlands 58-59, *58, 59*